Let's Stay in Touch

Please fill out this card and send it to us at Health Freedom Publications so that we can keep you posted on important health freedom issues.

Name:_____

Address:_____

City:_____ State:_____ Zip:_____

Phone number:_____

☐ Enclosed is $3.00. Please send me a legislative update the moment there has been any important changes in health freedom issues.

☐ I am interested in receiving notification of future health freedom publications.

☐ Please send me _____ additional copies of *STOP the FDA: Save Your Health Freedom.* I have enclosed $9.95 plus $3 for shipping and handling for each copy (California residents add 72¢ sales tax for each copy).

The following questions are optional, answer only if you feel comfortable.

Are you a health professional? ☐ Yes ☐ No

What is your line of work? _____

What is your yearly household income?
     ☐ 0-20K ☐ 20-40K ☐ 40-100K ☐ 100K+

What is your age? ☐ 0-20 ☐ 20-40 ☐ 40-65 ☐ 65+

Would you be interested in subscribing to a legislative update service on health freedom issues? ☐ Yes ☐ No

Do you take nutritional supplements regularly? ☐ Yes ☐ No

What supplements are most important to you?_____

_____

Other Comments:_____

_____

_____

_____

Health Freedom Publications
PO Box 2515
Menlo Park, CA 94026

Health Freedom Publications
PO Box 2515
Menlo Park, CA 94026

STOP the FDA:
Save Your Health Freedom

A Health Freedom Book

Edited by:
John Morgenthaler
and
Steven Wm. Fowkes

Health Freedom Publications
Menlo Park, California
1992

Notice: Please Read This First

The opinions expressed by the authors of the articles in this book are their own and do not necessarily reflect the opinions of the Editors. The scientific and medical information presented in these pages is for informational purposes only. It should **not** be used as a *substitute* for medical advice.

STOP the FDA: Save Your Health Freedom

Edited by John Morgenthaler & Steven Wm. Fowkes

A collection articles, some of which are original to this book, and some of which are reprinted here with permission.

Reprint permissions, where applicable, are listed at the end of each chapter.

Published by:
Health Freedom Publications
PO Box 2515, Menlo Park, CA 94026

Second Printing: 1992
Printed in the United States of America

John Morgenthaler & Steven Wm. Fowkes (editors)
STOP the FDA: Save Your Health Freedom
Second Edition
ISBN: 0-9627418-8-4: $9.95 Softcover

Table of Contents

Preface to New Edition

Many of the articles in this book refer to pending legislation by the 1992 bill numbers. As of June 1993, three "health freedom" bills have been introduced in Congress: 1) The Health Freedom Act of 1993 (HR 509), introduced by Representative Elton Gallegly (R-CA), 2) The Dietary Supplement Health and Education Act (S 784), introduced by Senator Orrin Hatch (R-UT), and 3) The Dietary Supplement Health and Education Act (HR 1709), introduced by Representative Bill Richardson (D-NM). Some of the provisions of these bills are similar, others are quite different. Many of these provisions will change as they are amended and/or compromised. Ongoing commentary on these bills is available from the health advocacy groups listed on page 185.

Notice: Please Read This First

The opinions expressed by the authors of the articles in this book are their own and do not necessarily reflect the opinions of the Editors. The scientific and medical information presented in these pages is for informational purposes only. It should **not** be used as a *substitute* for medical advice.

Authors Listing

Stop the FDA: Save Your Health Freedom

Introduction

Over the last few years, American citizens have been bombarded with news stories from around the world about political revolutions against authoritarian governmental institutions. In a graphic visual testament, the prototypical symbol of the "cold war," the Berlin Wall, was literally torn down in front of billions of TV viewers. In a development that surprised even conservatives, The Soviet Union has dissolved into its component states. On a worldwide basis, it appears that freedom is undergoing a rebirth.

Juxtaposed to this trend, the Food and Drug Administration, under the inspired leadership of the "enforcement Commissioner" David Kessler, MD, has carried out an unprecedented and systematic campaign to control the food, vitamin, nutrient, and medical decisions of United States citizens. To some readers — those on the receiving end of FDA enforcement actions — the previous sentence is an understatement. Picture instead: black leather boots kicking down doors; automatic weapons drawn and aimed at doctors, nurses, patients, business owners, employees, and customers; repeated raids intended to discourage cooperation with the press; self-serving press conferences with career-minded bureaucrats congratulating their own actions — all this smacks of totalitarian political tactics.

To many Americans, these scenes are completely unbelievable. This isn't the "freedom and opportunity" that we were taught about America in school. This isn't what we read in the Constitution. This isn't what our forefathers envisioned when they created the government for which we vote. To such readers, we apologize. The political content of this book may be ugly and upsetting. The behind-the-scenes maneuvering of some lawmakers reek of political favoritism. The special interests aligned on the sidelines have multi-billions of dollars in profits at stake. And the bottom line, for us, is no less than our freedom to choose the kinds of foods, supplements and health products we want. Our health, our lives, our welfare, our pursuit of happiness, have all become chips on some political poker table.

This book is intended as a partial solution. It contains information from widely different points of view on health, medicine and nutrient supplements. It also contains information on pending legislation that will either make the situation worse (the FDA Enforcement Bill) or make it better (the Health Freedom Acts). We hope that readers will become empowered to take action, action involving letters to legislators, phone calls, and votes — action that will clearly establish health freedom as the wish of the American people, in the courts, and in the minds of our politicians.

There have been many changes over the last half-century. The nutrient supplement industry has grown from a fledgling enterprise into a multi-billion dollar industry. During the same time, the health food industry has established increasing scientific respectability. Nutrients are now clearly recognized as significant protectors against heart disease and cancer. Nutrients are now considered the treatments-of-choice for several diseases.

Twenty years ago, scientists who engaged in nutrient-based pharmaceutical research were risking their grants and their careers. Today, scientists *can* choose to base their life-work on nutrients. Twenty years ago, the FDA wanted to censor *Psychology Today* and *Scientific American* to stop stories about the superior sleep-inducing properties of L-tryptophan. Last year, the FDA kept tryptophan off the US market without any scientific justification — and next year (1993), they plan to make "third party" claims about nutrients illegal (the NLEA regulations). Twenty years ago, claims that nutrients could prevent disease were considered quackery. Today, they are actually being made by federal agencies such as the Federal Trade Commission (FTC) and the National Cancer Institute (NCI). Today, the FDA is alone among federal institutions in its anti-vitamin, anti-nutrient, anti-health agenda.

Frankly, the American public deserves better.

Each of the following chapters has been collected or submitted by people in many different walks of life. Some are PhDs and MDs, some are lay people; some are famous, some are not; some are politically active, others are therapists. Each contribution offers a unique opinion and insight into a part of the American health system currently under siege.

E. G. Ross is a cartoonist-for-hire (looking for a syndicator). 1633 Best Lane, Eugene, OR 97401. Phone: 503-345-9379.

Statement of Senator Orrin Hatch before the US Senate: Introduction of the Health Freedom Act of 1992

From the Office of Senator Orrin Hatch, Washington, DC

This article is a reprint of Senator Hatch's introduction of the Health Freedom Act of 1992, S 2835, followed by an explanation of the act (also from Senator Hatch).

Mr. President, I am introducing today the "Health Freedom Act of 1992." After hearing from constituents in my home state of Utah, including both consumers and manufacturers of dietary supplement products, I strongly believe that this new legislation will help protect dietary supplements from unnecessary regulation.

There is a growing body of research that indicates that dietary supplements can help promote health and prevent certain diseases. In our free market system, consumers should be able to purchase dietary supplements, and companies should be free to sell these products so long as the labeling and advertising is truthful and non-misleading and there exists a reasonable scientific basis for product claims.

Dietary supplements are purchased because many consumers want to add supplemental quantities of vitamins, minerals, herbs, and other similar food substances to their ordinary or usual diet. Common examples of such products include vitamin C tablets, multi-vitamin/multi-mineral supplements, and capsules that provide herbs or fish oil.

In our free society, consumers should be able to purchase any food they want — whether it is an egg, ice cream, a steak, coffee, potato chips, or a dietary supplement — regardless of whether someone in the federal bureaucracy approves. Unfortunately, however, some people in the government, including some people at the US Food and Drug Administration (FDA), appear to have unfairly treated dietary supplements and have tried to establish unreasonable regulatory burdens on such products. For example, the FDA readily allows people to eat conventional food products that may be high in saturated fat, cholesterol, caffeine, sodium, or calories, or lacking in important vitamins or minerals. Yet the agency raises regulatory objections over safe dietary supplements of food substances that are desired by many consumers and that may be recommended by nutritionists or other health professionals. The Health Freedom Act of 1992 would correct this situation in several important ways.

Definition of "Dietary Supplement"

First, this bill provides a definition of the class of products to which it applies. It would define a dietary supplement as an article that includes, and is intended to supplement the diet with, a vitamin, a mineral, an herb, or another similar nutritional substance, including a concentrate or an extract of such a substance.

Dietary Supplements Are Not Drugs

Next, the bill provides that a dietary supplement shall not be considered a drug solely because of the potency of a substance in the supplement. This provision, in essence, would extend to all dietary supplements, a principle that section 411 of the FDC Act (commonly known as the Proxmire Amendments) has already established for vitamins and minerals — i.e., that FDA may not classify a food substance as a drug solely because it exceeds the level of potency that FDA believes is nutritionally rational or useful [21 USC S 350(a)(1)(b)].

This legislation also provides that a dietary supplement shall not be deemed to be a drug solely because the labeling or advertising for the supplement provides information concerning the potency of a substance in the supplement. This a logical extension of the point described above — that is, neither (1) the potency nor (2) truthful information in labeling or advertising *about* the potency of a safe substance in a dietary supplement should cause that supplement to be deemed to be a drug.

The bill also clarifies that a dietary supplement shall not be considered to be a drug solely because the labeling or advertising for the supplement contains a health claim of the type permitted by the new legislation.

Dietary Supplements Are Not Food Additives

My legislation states that a food substance provided by a dietary supplement is *not* subject to regulation by FDA as a "food additive," provided that the substance is identified in the labeling of the supplement as being provided by the product.

I believe food additive status for ingredients in dietary supplements should be reserved for chemical preservatives, sequestrants, emulsifiers, solvents, processing aids, or other such technical or functional agents. Indeed, I understand that these kinds of additives are often not used at all in dietary supplements. FDA should not be allowed to assert "food additive" requirements to prevent consumers from obtaining safe vitamins, minerals, herbs, or other similar *food* substances that they knowingly *want* to consume and to add to their diets by means of a dietary supplement.

This is not just a theoretical concern. For example, FDA has asserted that compounds of chromium are "unapproved food additives" and thus *illegal* when added to dietary supplements, even though it is clear that chromium is an *essential mineral* that (1) is *extremely safe* (in the trivalent form commonly used in dietary supplements) and (2) is not present in optimum amounts of all American diets. (See the National Academy of Sciences, *Recommended Dietary Allowances* (10th ed., 1989, pp. 241-243) for a review of the safety and usefulness of trivalent chromium.)

Chromium is currently found in many dietary supplement products, including major national brands of multi-vitamin/multi-mineral products such as "Centrum," "One-A-Day," "Theragran-N," and "Geritol," as well as in numerous other dietary supplement products sold in health food stores. The FDA should not be allowed to prevent consumers from obtaining chromium or supplements of other safe food substances by asserting that such foods are "food additives."

It is important to note that preventing the FDA from regulating food substances in dietary supplements as "food additives" does *not* deprive the FDA of ample authority to protect consumers from unsafe products. Section 402(a)(1) of the FDC Act, 21 USC section 342(a)(1), would continue to apply to dietary supplements. This section prohibits a food (including a dietary supplement) from bearing or containing any "poisonous or deleterious substance which may render it injurious to health." Under this section of the FDC Act, however, FDA must have some basis to show that a food substance is poisonous or deleterious and may render a product injurious to health before the agency can deprive consumers of foods that they want to purchase and consume — and that is just as it should be in a free society.

Truthful Health Information Permitted

My bill also provides that labeling or advertising about a dietary supplement may include claims or other information concerning the relationship of the supplement, or of one or more substances provided by the supplement, or of the absence of one or more of these substances, to a disease or health-related condition, *provided*, that such claims or other information are truthful and not misleading, *and*, that there is scientific evidence, whether published or unpublished, that provides a reasonable basis for such claims or other information.

As I observed recently when we passed the Nutrition Labeling and Education Act,

> *"By their very nature, the dietary supplements must be marketed so that the consumer is informed of the health or disease-prevention benefits that may be conferred. Greater flexibility is thus required to permit communication of these benefits. This increased regulatory flexibility is also mandated by the very rapid pace of scientific advances here and abroad linking the prevention of long-term disease to improved nutritional supplementation.*

For these reasons, a more lenient standard of dietary supplements is envisioned."
Congressional Record — Senate, p. S16611 (October 24, 1990)

Nevertheless, after passage of that Act, FDA has tried to impose severe restraints on the freedom of dietary supplement manufacturers to provide truthful disease- and health-related information in labeling [56 Fed. Reg. 60537, November 27, 1992]. The new Health Freedom Act of 1992 would correct this situation and clearly *permit* such information in labeling or advertising, *provided* that the information is truthful and not misleading *and* that there is reasonable scientific basis for the information. I believe this is a standard that most Americans would readily support.

No Prior Restraints by FDA on Truthful Labeling or Advertising

Furthermore, the Health Freedom Act of 1992 would provide that FDA shall *not* establish any requirement that disease- or health-related claims or other information concerning a dietary supplement must be approved by or conform to a regulation issued by FDA before they may be used in labeling or advertising. This provision is needed because FDA has recently proposed regulations that would *not* allow *any* disease- or health-related information (including truthful information) to be provided in labeling for dietary supplements until FDA first issues a regulation approving the information [56 Fed. Reg 60537, November 27, 1991]. If a labeling claim is made that is false or misleading, or if there is otherwise no reasonable basis for a claim, FDA has, and would continue to have, ample authority to take action against the subject product, as a misbranded food [21 USC section 343(a)]. Petitions for FDA to issue regulations can be extremely time-consuming and costly to prepare, and it typically takes FDA three to five years to issue a new regulation. Health- and disease-related information about food substances should not be subject to such burdensome and delaying prior restraints. Furthermore, enforcement convenience for FDA should not be given priority over freedom of commercial speech.

Right to Judicial Review
of FDA Warning Letters

Finally, this legislation would provide that if FDA issues a warning letter concerning a dietary supplement, asserting that a disease- or health-related claim is false or misleading or that there is insufficient scientific evidence to support the claim, the manufacturer or other responsible party may seek direct judicial review of the merits of FDA's assertion. FDA currently maintains that when it issues a warning letter to a dietary supplement company, the company cannot test the validity of the agency's allegations by seeking immediate court review. The new law would be clear that this is not the case.

Mr. President, I believe this bill is reasonable and proper and will be welcomed by all Americans, and should be supported by senators of both parties, regardless of whether they are consumers of dietary supplement products. In our free society, consumers should be able to purchase dietary supplements, and companies should be free to sell such substances to consumers, with truthful and non-misleading labeling and advertising information that is supported by a reasonable scientific basis, *without* undue governmental interference with the free flow of such products and information. Accordingly, I strongly encourage all of my colleagues in the Senate to give their support to the Health Freedom Act of 1992.

I ask unanimous consent that a summary and section-by-section analysis of the bill be inserted in the Record immediately following my remarks.

Thank you, Mr. President.

Editor's note: *This is the end of Senator Hatch's address to the Senate. His summary of the Health Freedom Act of 1992 — S 1992 — begins on the following page.*

Summary of the
Health Freedom Act of 1992

The purpose of the Health Freedom Act of 1992 is to help assure that consumers who wish to purchase dietary supplements such as vitamins, minerals and herbs may do so in a framework that allows consumers the maximum amount of choice in the marketplace while retaining a proper level of public health safeguards.

There is a growing body of research that indicates that dietary supplements can help promote health and prevent certain diseases. In a free market system, consumers should be able to purchase supplemental quantities of safe food substances, and companies should be free to sell these supplements so long as the product labeling and advertising is truthful and non-misleading and there exists a reasonable scientific basis for product claims.

The Health Freedom Act of 1992 defines dietary supplements as articles that supplement the diet with vitamins, minerals, herbs, or other similar nutritional substances, including concentrates or extracts. The Act provides that a dietary supplement shall not be considered to be a drug solely because of the potency of a substance in the dietary supplement or because its labeling bears a health claim authorized by the Act or provides information about the potency of the dietary supplement.

Under the provisions of the Act, a food substance provided by a dietary supplement cannot be considered a food additive if it is identified in the labeling. Dietary supplements remain subject to the safety provisions of section 402(a)(1) of the Federal Food, Drug and Cosmetic Act [21 USC 342(a)(1)].

The Health Freedom Act of 1992 establishes a new section 413 of the Federal Food, Drug and Cosmetic Act entitled, "Labeling and Advertising of Dietary Supplements." Under new section 413, health claims are permitted for dietary supplements that are, (1) truthful and not misleading, and (2) supported by scientific evidence, whether published or unpublished, that provides a reasonable basis for such claims. The Food and Drug Administration is prohibited from establishing pre-clearance requirements for such health claims.

If the Food and Drug Administration challenges a health claim as false, misleading or not scientifically valid, the responsible company may seek a declaratory judgment in the appropriate federal court. A company's decision not to seek judicial review shall not result in an inference that the Food and Drug Administration's assertion is valid. The burden of proof shall continue to rest upon the Food and Drug Administration to demonstrate that the health claim fails to meet the standard of evidence set forth under the Act.

The Health Freedom Act of 1992 repeals the provision of the Nutrition Labeling and Education Act that permits the Food and Drug Administration to establish a procedure and standard respecting the validity of disease- or health-related claims for dietary supplements because the new Act provides specific standards to govern such supplements.

Both the Statement of Senator Orrin Hatch before the US Senate: Introduction of the Health Freedom Act of 1992, S 2835 and the Bill Summary: The "Health Freedom Act of 1992, S 2835" were prepared by the Office of Senator Orrin Hatch in Washington, DC.

As bills are submitted for consideration, they are assigned a number. The Health Freedom Act of 1992 was designated Senate Bill 2835, or S.B. 2835, or S 2835, for short. In the House, bills are referred to as "House Resolutions", or H.R. or HR for short. Throughout this book, we use the most compact 'S' and 'HR' abbreviations.

The Health Freedom Act will be assigned a new number when it is resubmitted in the 1993 Senate.

Nutrition: At the Crossroads

Brian Leibovitz, PhD

Dr. Brian Leibovitz holds an MS degree in biology from Portland State University (in conjunction with the University of Oregon Medical School) and a PhD in zoology and physiology from the University of Wyoming. He was a research associate to Nobel Prize Laureate, Dr. Linus Pauling, and completed his post-doctoral research in the Department of Food Science and Technology at the University of California at Davis. Dr. Leibovitz has published numerous scientific articles in the field of nutrition, and the book Carnitine *(Dell, 1984). Dr. Leibovitz is the Editor-in-Chief of the* Journal of Optimal Nutrition *and has a nutritional consulting practice in Davis, California. He writes* Nutrition Update *and three columns in* Muscular Development. *He is currently engaged in writing an updated edition of his book and co-authoring the Second Edition of* How to Live Longer and Feel Better *with Dr. Linus Pauling.*

The future is what we make it, and is molded by today's thoughts and tomorrow's actions. As I see it, nutrition is at a crucial junction from which there are two possible directions: 1) one in which nutrients are extensively used to prevent and treat human diseases, and 2) one in which the therapeutic applications of nutritional supplements continue to be ignored.

I started this article with the intention of discussing all the players, concepts, and events. There is simply too much to cover, however, and some of the topics will have to wait for future issues.

No Vested Interests

Although often stated, it always bears repeating that I do not profit from product sales. Although I am the Scientific and Nutritional Consultant for Twin Laboratories, Inc., I am *not*, and have *never* been, financially rewarded from the sale of any nutrient or products. I receive no bonuses, no stock, no percentages, no perks of any kind.

Equally important, I am *not* required (nor have I ever been asked) to write or speak about any nutrient or product which, in my opinion, lacks sufficient documentation. Consequently, I have no vested interests whatsoever, which allows me to maintain objectivity. Those who are familiar with the health food industry know how very rare this relationship really is.

My only goal is to help speed the day when nutritional supplements are used to the fullest extent possible to reduce the morbidity and mortality of human diseases, and to improve the quality of life.

Crisis in the Health Care System

There is little doubt that the health care system is in serious trouble, and both public and private sectors have been hurt by escalating medical costs that far exceed the rate of inflation. Expensive, high-tech equipment, unnecessary operations, and superfluous diagnostic tests all contribute to the problem. Yet as bad off as the health care system is financially, things are even worse in the area of therapeutic efficacy.

Lost in the Forest

"If it isn't broken, don't fix it," states the age-old adage. Conversely, if the system is obviously broken, it's time for repairs. The medically approved drugs used for treating a number of diseases are often so ill-conceived, and present such great health hazards, as to warrant a major overhaul of the system. This is particularly true for drugs used in treating chronic, age-associated disorders; the majority are either ineffective or toxic; many drugs are both. Sidney Harris eloquently expressed this in a cartoon in which a patient told his doctor that 'he had stopped taking the drug, as he preferred the original disease to the side effects.' One need only look at *The New England Journal of Medicine* (*NEJM*), *The Journal of the American Medical Association* (*JAMA*) or any other medical journal to discover this awful truth. And you don't need to look for very long.

Heartless Medicines

Drugs used for treating cardiovascular diseases are, by-and-large, essentially worthless (albeit these drugs are an effective means of population control). A classic example was published in the November 21, 1991 issue of *NEJM*. This article was about a double-blind, randomized, multi-center trial of milrinone (a drug which inhibits *phosphodiesterase*) in 1,088 patients with severe chronic heart failure.[1]

> *Compared to placebo, milrinone therapy resulted in a 28 percent increase in mortality from all causes (P=0.038) and a 34 percent increase in cardiovascular mortality (P=0.016).*

Furthermore, milrinone significantly increased the number of serious adverse *cardiovascular* reactions and also hospitalizations as compared with the placebo group.[1] Nice drug!

An increase in mortality after treatment with cardiac drugs is the rule, not the exception. Consider the drug clofibrate, a lipid-lowering drug prescribed for millions of men world-wide. In a six-year, World Health Organization (WHO) study of 5,000 patients with known coronary heart disease, clofibrate treatment resulted in a 44% higher mortality rate as compared to placebo.[2]

Side Effects. In addition to higher mortality rates, most cardiac drugs produce a plethora of harmful side-effects. Consider the drug Plendil (felodipine), a calcium channel blocker. In the latest issue of *NEJM*, an advertisement for Plendil lists over 15 adverse reactions at a dose of 5 mg, including: peripheral edema (in 22% of patients), headache (in 19%), flushing (in 6%), dizziness (in 6%), upper respiratory infection (in 6%), and palpitation (in 2% of patients). Moreover, the toxicity of Plendil is dose-dependent: at 20 mg the incidence of peripheral edema is 36%, headache 28%, flushing 20%, and palpitation 12%. The advertisement also stated that Plendil's "safety in patients with heart failure has not been established."

Imagine the FDA's reaction to a nutrient that produced such an array of untoward side-effects! The FDA would undoubtedly deem it toxic and ban its sale. Recall that guar gum (a soluble fiber) was banned from weight-loss products by the FDA because *a few individuals* didn't dilute it properly and choked (the FDA never said how many people, nor did they mention the outcome).

It's no joke that the average drug advertisement has one sentence of indications followed by a full page (sometimes more) of contraindications, warnings, precautions, adverse reactions, and toxic effects.

Leaving drugs for a moment, other treatment modalities of modern cardiovascular medicine are even more deranged. Artificial hearts, for example, are even further removed from the ultimate management of cardiovascular diseases. In a recent review of the artificial heart program, a blue-ribbon panel from the Institute of Medicine concluded "the projected costs would be greater, and the benefits lower, than for any medical procedure now in use, but that research should go on anyway."[3]

The Curious Case of Cancer Chemotherapy

One of the most puzzling, unfathomable aspects of modern medicine is in the area of cancer chemotherapy, specifically, the justification behind the drugs currently prescribed. Virtually all anticancer drugs are carcinogens in their own right, a feature I've never been able to figure out.

These drugs, by-and-large, are the worst chemicals on the shelf; they work by damaging the DNA of fast-growing cells, thereby inhibiting growth potential. That's fine for tumor cells, but the indiscriminate toxicity of these anti-metabolites also obliterates cells in the gastrointestinal tract, bone marrow, mucous epithelium, hair, and the immune system (particularly those involved in anticancer and antimicrobial immunity). The non-specific nature of chemotherapy results in severe gastro-intestinal damage, malnutrition, anemia, loss of hair, and immune dysfunction. Naturally, death from bacterial or other infections is common in cancer patients given chemotherapy; estimates of infection as the proximate cause of death in cancer patients range from 50% (in those with solid tumors) to 75% (in leukemia patients).[4]

In a recently published review of the book *Cancer Risk After Medical Treatment*, Dr. Penn (the reviewer) observed that:

> *"It is one of the great paradoxes of medicine that the treatment of cancer may be complicated by the development of a second type of cancer induced by radiotherapy, chemotherapy, or both treatments. There is an increased risk of acute non-lymphocytic leukemia after treatment with a variety of alkylating agents and an increased risk of carcinoma of the bladder after treatment with cyclophosphamide."* [5]

In another article published recently in *NEJM*, continuous combination chemotherapy (cyclophosphamide, methotrexate, and fluorouracil) was compared to no treatment in 250 women with metastatic breast cancer.[6] The results: chemotherapy did not improve survival, but it did significantly decrease the quality of life (as evidenced by an increased frequency of vomiting, nausea, mucositis, and other "side-effects" of these noxious poisons).

Another class of chemotherapy agents is based on adriamycin (aka doxorubicin). Adriamycin works by redox [REDuction-OXidation] cycling, thereby generating copious quantities of free radicals which overwhelm defense systems of cancer cells, as well as cells in the heart. Not surprisingly, adriamycin is very cardiotoxic, and approximately 10-15% of cancer patients given this drug die from cardiomyopathy.[7] In fact, adriamycin is so effective (meaning cardiotoxic), it's become a favorite model system for many laboratories studying oxidative damage and antioxidants.

The bottom line is that the twenty-year, $22 billion dollar war on cancer has failed to produce any real benefits. As discussed in a recent issue of *Science*, "Overall death rates from many common cancers remain stubbornly unchanged — or even higher — than when the war began."[8] Dr. Samuel Epstein and 60 physicians and scientists — at a press conference in Washington, D.C. — charged that the cancer establishment repeatedly and grossly exaggerated its ability to treat and cure cancer:

> *"The cancer establishment confuses the public with repeated claims that we are winning the war.... Our*

ability to treat and cure most cancers has not materially improved."[9]

The Bitter Truth

The question which must be honestly addressed, and which has not heretofore even been asked is:

If the medications presently used to treat the major diseases were truly efficacious, then why are cardiovascular diseases, cancer, and lung diseases still the leading causes of death?

The cold, cruel fact is that — despite the highly proclaimed advancements in medicine — many hundreds of thousands of Americans die each year because they are given the wrong medicines. Aside from emergency medicine, diagnostics, orthopedics, and certain other specialties, modern medicine has simply missed the forest for the trees. I would be remiss in not mentioning a remarkable exception: the National Cancer Institute. NCI is currently supporting some 40 studies on the anticancer effects of a variety of nutrient supplements (vitamin A, beta-carotene, vitamin C, vitamin E, selenium, folic acid, and others).

Most other branches of medicine, however, have been slow to recognize the value of supplementation. This is particularly true of the heart-disease establishment, which is trapped in the dogma of polyunsaturated fatty acids (PUFAs) of the omega-6 series being of benefit in treating coronary heart disease. That fantasy, plus the idea that cholesterol *per se* is the cause of coronary artery disease, has been promulgated for so long, and with such fanaticism, that a retraction at this stage would involve a serious loss of credibility.

Scenario #1:
Nutrition as the
Foundation of Medicine

In this scenario, there will be an ever-increasing incorporation of nutritional supplements in the prevention and treatment of human diseases. Many, if not most, diseases will probably be successfully managed with dietary supplements of vitamins, minerals, and non-vitamin nutrients (e.g., coenzyme Q_{10}, L-carnitine, anthocyanins and other flavonoids, d-limonene and other terpenes, and carotenoids). In addition, macronutrient composition and quantity will be used for therapeutic benefit (e.g., the inhibition of platelet aggregation by fish oil supplements or the improvement in blood lipid profiles by supplementary fiber).

This prediction is based on several factors, the most important being the thousands of studies (published in respectable, peer-reviewed journals) which I've accumulated over the past 18 years. The volume of literature is incredibly large at present, and it's growing by leaps and bounds. I photocopy 10-30 articles on supplements each week at the UC Davis Health Sciences Library. My collection of articles on nutrition and disease now fills 38 metal file cabinets (two 5-stack, six 4-stack, and two 2-stack file cabinets — the 25"-deep kind).

I believe that nutrients — especially micronutrients — will be recognized as the medicines of choice, and that, ultimately, nutrients will supplant most drugs used in clinical medicine. The handwriting is clearly on the wall.

Most people think of nutritional supplements for the prevention of disease, which is fine, as substantial data have accumulated in support of this concept. In real life, however, most people wait for the lumps, bumps, aches, and pains: it is a rare individual who actually has the foresight to use supplements prophylactically. Nutritional supplementation as a therapeutic modality is at least as important as its preventive roles. This topic has begun to be studied in earnest, and results document the benefits of increasing dietary intakes of nutrients in the treatment as well as prevention of numerous human diseases.

Non-Vitamin Nutrients: The Gray Area. This interface between vitamins and natural products includes coenzyme Q_{10}, bioflavonoids, carotenoids, carnitine, and terpenes — compounds which belong to a group I call "non-vitamin nutrients."

These naturally occurring compounds are not considered vitamins (except for some pro-vitamin A carotenoids); nonetheless, numerous beneficial effects are elicited by dietary supplementation with these remarkable molecules. The volume of the data is really quite astounding: articles about carnitine fill an entire file cabinet, as do those about bioflavonoids and coenzyme Q_{10}. Carotenoid articles fill yet another.

Bioflavonoids are probably the hottest class of non-vitamin nutrients, and their medical applications span almost every pathology and organ. Silybin, a flavonolignin complex isolated from milk thistle, was chosen as the cover molecule for this inaugural issue of the *Journal of Optimal Nutrition*. In Europe, silybin is marketed as a drug for the treatment of cirrhosis. Like most bioflavonoids, it has potent antioxidant and metal-chelating properties; in addition, silybin raises liver glutathione levels.

Supplements: A "Radical" Concept?

The idea that optimal nutrition requires super-physiological amounts of the micronutrients is by no means a new concept. In 1938, Drs. Stepp, Kuhnau, and Schroeder published a book entitled *Vitamins and Their Clinical Applications* in which they stated the following:[10]

> *"The conception that the investigation of the pure vitamin might possibly disclose new and so far unknown effects has proven especially productive with vitamin C. It appears that this vitamin given in pure form may influence disease conditions, which (so much may be said today) have nothing to do with states of avitaminoses or hypovitaminoses. Thus, the vitamins, beyond the service they render as accessory substances, possess the properties of curative stuffs." [emphasis added].*

This is a good description of *JON*'s focus, namely, that dietary supplements of macronutrients and micronutrients are beneficial in the prevention and/or treatment of disease as well as in the maintenance of optimal health. So *JON*'s unique focus is really based on ideas conceived over a half a century ago. It is both a tribute to the early nutrition investigators and a reason for humility about the novelty of our conceptions.

The interest and excitement in this field is blossoming as ever before, as reflected by the present number of nutrition journals (> 35), books (> 50/year), and conferences (> 40/yr conservatively). The recent New York Academy of Sciences Conference entitled "Beyond Deficiency: New Views on The Function and Health Benefits of Vitamins" (chaired by Drs. Machlin and Sauberlich) is further confirmation of the growing interest in nutritional supplementation.

Time for a Change

Time Magazine recently published a lead article entitled "The New Scoop on Vitamins." [11] This cover story had a huge impact, and it is still being widely discussed. It was six pages in length, and, considering it was written for the general public, rather well done.

The article covered free radicals/antioxidants and cancer, heart disease, aging, cataracts, birth defects, infectious diseases, and a host of other diseases. In addition, folic acid supplementation as a means of preventing neural tube defects in children was discussed; as was folate's capacity to reverse precancerous lesions of the cervix. The increased requirement for vitamins and other nutrients with advancing age was also pointed out, as was the increased requirements for nutrients in persons taking various medications. The author hit the nail on the head in the summary statement:

> *"They [vitamins] may be much more important than doctors thought in warding off cancer, heart disease, and the ravages of aging — and no, you may not be getting enough of these crucial nutrients in your diet."*

The fact that *Time Magazine* went out on a limb with this provocative cover story indicates their lawyers felt the documentation was sufficient to protect against lawsuit. The *New York Times* also joined in with its article entitled "Vitamins Win Support as Potent Agents of Health" (March 10, 1992). These were soon followed by an article in *USA Today* entitled

"Megadose Vitamin C Linked to Longer Life" (May 8-10, 1992). The latter report (published in *Epidemiology*) was based on a study of 11,348 US adults, and revealed that men with the highest vitamin C intakes had a 35% lower mortality rate and a 42% lower death rate from heart disease and stroke (women had a 10% lower mortality rate and a 25% lower death rate from heart disease and stroke).

In fact, it seems everyone in the US knows that nutritional supplements can be of benefit in disease prevention and/or treatment. Even the conservative dietitian at CNN (Carolyn O'Neil) brought up this concept when she reported that calcium intakes above the RDA could benefit those with high blood pressure.

Yes, most Americans are aware of nutrients' potential health benefits — a concept whose time has indeed arrived. Most, that is, except those at the FDA who are entrusted with regulating the supplement industry.

Scenario #2:
A Dismal Future

In this doleful scenario, nutritional supplements would remain the unwanted stepchild of medicine. More importantly, medical policies would continue to be decided by financial or political considerations rather than scientific facts. In this future, many nutrients would be banned, others available only by prescription and in limited quantities. It goes without saying that costs would skyrocket, perhaps as much as tenfold over today's prices. Moreover, there would continue to be hundreds of thousands of needless deaths resulting from use of the wrong medicines (and from the lack of availability of nutrient supplements). There are many forces working to make Scenario #2 a reality. The remainder of this article details some of those forces and how they work.

The FDA Run Amok

The FDA has, for all intents and purposes, been running amok, and it's already claimed two victims: America's public health and the integrity of science. The ban on L-tryptophan, the upcoming Dietary Supplement Task Force report by Associate Commissioner Dykstra (in which all amino acids are to be banned from over-the-counter sale), the switch from RDA to the worthless "RDI," the institution of a bogus protein-quality measurement (the so-called "PDCAAS," see below) to sell a type of protein, and SWAT-team-style arrests of physicians working in their clinics are just a few examples.

If It Works, It's a Drug

There is a legal "Catch 22" in the supplement industry resulting from current regulations. If a nutrient or food factor is *well documented* to be therapeutically effective, the FDA will probably label it a drug and ban its OTC [over-the-counter] sale. If it is effective, but the data are not *unequivocal*, the FDA can nail you for marketing an approved "drug" without following proper procedure (e.g., filing a New Drug Application). Conversely, they could also cite you for marketing an unapproved food substance for the treatment of disease. It's a case of where you just can't win for trying.

Even stranger is that *ineffective* OTC supplements never seem to get noticed or hassled, such as diosgenin, gamma-oryzanol, Smilax, and other plant sterols which are marketed as anabolic agents. These ideas gave rise to the following principle:

> **The stronger the data supporting the efficacy of a nutritional supplement, the sooner it will be banned from over-the-counter sales.**

> **Corollary:** *The drug derivative, however, will soon be widely acclaimed for its therapeutic value.*

The B-Vitamin Bust: Did FDA Wrong Wright?

On May 6 [1992], a raiding party of six FDA agents attacked the clinic of Jonathan Wright, MD, in Kent, Washington. With guns drawn and wearing flak jackets, they broke down the door and — SWAT-team style — stormed the clinic. And just in case (in case of what I still can't figure out), the FDA had a backup of 10 local police. They pointed their guns at both staff and patients in an obvious (and probably successful) attempt to harass and intimidate. This lasted for some time, after which FDA agents removed many office items (e.g., supplements, records, files, and medical equipment). Apparently, the FDA also raided a nearby pharmacy and medical laboratory at the same time. The increased number, and ferocity, of FDA raids might well be a prelude to further restrictions on the OTC availability of nutritional supplements. Indeed, the FDA recently hired approximately 100 enforcement agents, presumably for such purposes. If the incident in Kent, Washington, is any indication, we won't have long to wait.

What was the heinous crime that led to this raid? Did Dr. Wright commit rape, child abuse, or murder? Was he selling crack or cheating on his income tax? Nope. *Dr. Wright's crime was simply the possession of vitamins*, specifically, an injectable mixture of B complex vitamins. If this is difficult to fathom, or evokes feelings of anger and frustration, relax. You're in good company. Intelligent people throughout the US were, and continue to be, baffled by these unexplainable, objectionable, and possibly unlawful actions of the FDA.

What If.... Imagine being arrested for possession of L-carnitine. Or six months hard labor for N-acetylcysteine, or L-arginine. Because its benefits are so well-documented, possession of coenzyme Q_{10} would probably get you two to four years in the Federal Penitentiary, assuming it was your first offense.

Where would it stop? We'd have to purchase our nutrients from shady characters on dark street corners. Of course, a black market would develop, with drug czars and all. Crime usually follows lucrative, illicit enterprises, so the number of murders and muggings would be bound to rise. The "vitamin pushers," once arrested, would further overcrowd our already overflowing jails. On Wall Street, the market would certainly suffer from the loss of US dollars to foreign "vitamin kingpins." More police would have to be hired to assist the overburdened "supplement police," and the army would likely get diverted from the war on drugs to the war on vitamins. Naturally, taxes would have to be raised to pay for all this. And so on. This all sounds pretty silly until you realize that the FDA is well on its way to implementing such a plan.

The "Great Vitamin War." The arrest of Dr. Wright did produce one unexpected *benefit*: it shocked us into doing something. Suddenly, people realized that action must be taken, and soon, to protect our rights to the unrestricted availability of nutrients and food factors, and to prevent FDA's strangulation of the supplement industry. The "Great Vitamin War," as it has been called, is on. In a way, after so many years of "cold war," the recent declaration is almost a relief.

Tryptophan, EMS, and the FDA

The FDA has *already* removed one nutrient from the OTC market. In late 1989, the FDA recalled virtually all L-tryptophan-containing products following the deaths of several dozen people from EMS [Eosinophilia Myalgia Syndrome]. EMS is a rare disorder which is characterized by abnormally high blood eosinophil counts, influenza-like symptoms, and by muscular pain.

The first breakthrough in understanding EMS came in July 1990, when EMS was firmly linked to L-tryptophan from a single manufacturer (Showa Denko — a large Japanese chemical and pharmaceutical company).[12] Later studies revealed that suspect batches of L-tryptophan from Showa Denko contained an impurity which might be the cause of EMS. This impurity was isolated by high-performance liquid chromatography [HPLC] as "peak E," which was suggested to be the dl-tryptophan aminal in acetaldehyde (DTAA).[13] More recently, chemical and spectral studies have demonstrated that "peak E" is a tryptophan derivative called 1,1'-ethylidenebis-[tryptophan].[14]

The presence of this toxic impurity has been linked to the use of a new, genetically recombined strain of bacteria (*bacillus amyloliquefaciens*, Strain V) in Showa Denko's lots of tryptophan produced between October 1988 and June 1989.[15] In addition, the toxic contaminant has been attributed to several changes in the purification procedures which were instituted during the time period in question. This former point raises serious concerns about the use of recombinant bacteria in fermentation technology. The FDA apparently did not learn the lesson of EMS, namely, that recombinant genetic techniques can produce novel toxins in our nutrient (or food) supply. If EMS was caused by consumption of gram quantities of genetically recombined material (L-tryptophan supplements), what may happen when kilogram quantities of recombinant vegetables are eaten?

Be that as it may, the bottom line is that L-tryptophan *per se* is not the cause of EMS. This disease is due to the presence of a contaminant which resulted from inappropriate production and inadequate purification procedures.[16] Clearly, production and purity standards need to be defined and implemented so that this kind of industrial mistake never happens again. With proper quality control protocols, there is no reason not to lift the ban.

To retain the ban on L-tryptophan supplements, however, is absurd in light of the fact that L-tryptophan is used every day in every US hospital in total parenteral nutrition (TPN) solutions. TPN is given intravenously, and hence purity is even more critical than for oral supplements. If L-tryptophan is allowed for use in TPN solutions (where it is used as the free amino acid), then it would most certainly be safe given by the oral route.

And a final comment: L-tryptophan occurs in many foods, particularly protein-rich foods like steak and milk; humans consume 1-2 grams per day in the average diet. Should the FDA consider

DECADES OF DOCUMENTED SUPPLEMENT BENEFITS

BENEFITS? HUH? WHAT BENEFITS? I DON'T SEE ANY BENEFITS!

FDA

banning steak, milk, cheese or other foods rich in L-trypto-phan? This argument is a *reductio ad absurdum*, but it does serve to illustrate the inherent fallacy in the FDA's indictment of L-tryptophan.

The crucial point is that an amino acid (or other nutrient) which is essential for life in a given, nutritional quantity cannot, by definition, be toxic when consumed in such amounts.

Don't Confuse Them With Facts

What really boggles the mind is that the FDA, Victor Herbert, and a few others in the nutrition community actually continue to deny the existence of *any* convincing data on the use of therapeutic applications of nutritional supplements. Such a stance flies in the face of overwhelming evidence to the contrary, and is as hard to comprehend as the denial of the holocaust.

What I'd really like to know is: *how do they avoid seeing any of the thousands of articles published in the scientific literature?* It must be a very special talent: only the FDA, Victor Herbert, Stephen Barrett, Frederick Stare, Richard Wurtman, and a handful of others believe that nutrient supplements are worth-less except for treating nutritional deficiencies. It is very doubt-ful that one could spend 10 minutes in any Health Sciences Library periodicals room and *not* find at least one article about nutritional supplements benefiting some disease or condition.

In the summer of 1991, while Editor-in-Chief of *The Journal of Applied Nutrition*, I wrote to Dr. Kessler, Gary Dykstra, and Dr. Vanderveen (Head of Nutrition at FDA) about joining my Editorial Board. By autumn, I'd sent two letters and made dozens of follow-up calls to each of these FDA officials. In addition, I offered to send complimentary copies of all the nutrition articles I could find in my weekly sojourns to the library. Not a bad offer, considering the large number of articles I always end up with.

Only Mr. Dykstra had the courtesy to respond to the Editorial Board invitation (he declined, of course). And none responded to my offer of free copies of the latest nutritional literature. Evidently, these top FDA officials aren't interested in learning about what they're regulating.

My experiences only confirm what most Americans already know: *The FDA is apparently not interested in an honest evaluation of the overwhelming amount of documentation regarding medical applications of nutritional supplements.*

The RDI: From Bad to Worthless

The FDA has proposed a new food labeling standard for vitamins and minerals called the "Reference Daily Intake" (RDI). The RDI is intended to replace the existing US RDA, and is a part of the broader National Labeling and Education Act (NLEA) passed in 1990. RDIs *will go into effect without the approval of any other branch of government and without review by any scientific body on November 8, 1992* [emphasis added].

If you think the RDAs are bad, wait until you see the RDIs! First off, there is only one RDI value for any nutrient, regardless of age, sex, or pregnancy/lactation. Worse, the RDIs are significantly lower than the RDAs (by 10-40%) for 16 nutrients. Biotin is down 40%, calcium by 25%, magnesium by 25%, vitamin A by 12%, thiamine (B_1) by 20%, vitamin B_6 by 25%, and so on. A comparison of RDA and RDI values for selected nutrients is provided in Table 1.

Table 1. The RDAs and RDIs of Selected Nutrients.

Nutrient	1989 RDA[†]	Proposed "Reference Daily Intake" (RDI)	Percent Decrease
Vitamin A	1,000 RE[‡]	875 RE	12
Vitamin D	10 mcg	6.5 mcg	35
Vitamin E	10 αTE[§]	9 αTE	10
Vitamin B_6	2 mg	1.5 mg	25
Biotin	100 mcg	60 mcg	40
Magnesium	400 mg	300 mg	25
Phosphorous	1,200 mg	900 mg	25

† Highest 1989 RDA.   ‡ Retinol equivalents.   § α-tocopherol equivalents.

Switching from RDAs (already low) to RDIs is analogous to reducing the definition of poverty to annual incomes of less than $1,000. The poor would cease to exist on paper, but in reality nothing would change. With the RDIs, dietary deficiencies may cease to exist simply because of how they are defined. More information on the RDI may be found in Dr. Jeff Blumberg's article [Nutrition Labeling Standards and the Future of Nutrition, *The Journal of Optimal Nutrition* 1(1): 43-45, 1992].

Confusion as a Weapon: The RDI, DRV, and PDV

One tactic of the FDA is to confuse and befuddle. If enough three-letter acronyms are introduced, the general public gets confused and quits trying to understand nutrient intakes. This is, in my opinion, one reason for the FDA's introduction of the RDI. And more recently, the FDA revealed another three-letter acronym: the Daily Reference Value (DRV).[17] This is the only place I've seen the DRV mentioned, and in this article DRV was not even defined! The article referred to DRV only once, and stated that: "the proposed FDA collective term for RDI and DRV is 'Percent of Daily Value'." Like the DRV, the "Percent of Daily Value" [PDV] was not defined.

It's almost laughable, like a Charlie Chaplin movie; we have, in addition to the RDA, the RDI, DRV, and now the PDV. I'd like to add one more: Generally Regarded As True (GRAT). The FDA needs to learn that, despite the RDA, RDI, DRV, PDV, GRAS [Generally Recognized As Safe] or PDCAAS (see below), the therapeutic benefits of supplementary nutrients are GRAT.

However humorous this may seem, their strategy works. Make no mistake about it: the public, confused and bewildered by all these acronyms, simply gives up trying to understand nutrition.

Science by Proclamation: The PDCAAS

The FDA has really hit a new low with the PDCAAS — the "Protein Digestibility Corrected Amino Acid Score." The PDCAAS was described in the same recent article as were the DRV and PDV.[17] Basically, the FDA plans to redefine how protein quality is measured. They argue that the PER (Protein

Efficiency Ratio), being done in rats, is not a good measure; yet the Protein Digestibility (PD) part of the PDCAAS is determined using a rat assay!

It gets worse. The FDA plans to set soy protein at a PDCAAS of 1.0 — the top of the PDCAAS rating scale. More important, they state that:

> *"If a food has a PDCAAS above 1.0, then it shall be set at 1.0."* [17]

In other words, all higher-quality proteins (e.g., lactalbumin, egg albumin, fish, or casein) will, by the FDA's definition, be equal to soy protein.

The only exception is infant foods, where the PER will be retained and required for labeling purposes. The FDA must have realized that they'd have a lot of dead babies on their hands if they allowed the PDCAAS to replace the PER in infant formulas. Infants need higher-quality protein than soy can supply.

Incidentally, the article was written by Dr. E. C. Henley, Director of Nutritional Science at Protein Technologies International, Checkerboard Square, St. Louis. And the FDA's decision to change the determination of protein quality was in response to a "citizen petition submitted by Protein Technologies International, Inc. (Docket No. 90P-0052)."[17] Could Ralston-Purina be looking to sell some soy protein? Soy is a good protein, to be sure, but it will never be as high-quality as lactalbumin — no matter what its PDCAAS rating.

If the FDA is ever allowed to change science to sell product — the ultimate prostitution of science — we are all in deep trouble.

Nutraceuticals, Nutritionists, and Nature

There are several key concepts that need to be mentioned, but because of space considerations, the discussions will be brief.

Nutrients as Drugs: The Patent Game

Why does it seem like nutrient supplements are dismissed as worthless by both the orthodox medical community as well as some nutritionists? And why has the acceptance of the clinical value of nutritional supplements been so agonizingly slow, despite the enormous volume of scientific documentation? If truth be told, it is money. The fact is, nutrients are non-patentable; without such protection, the pharmaceutical industry has very little incentive to investigate nutrients.

In contrast, therapeutic *applications* of nutritional supplements are patentable (so-called "use patents"). Several nutritional entrepreneurs hold a number of these, but the "King" of use patents has to be Dr. Richard Wurtman, a professor at the Massachusetts Institute of Technology. A recent search of US patents revealed that Dr. Wurtman owns over 20 use patents on various medical applications of supplementary amino acids. Some examples include: L-tyrosine for increasing blood pressure (US Patent #4,745,130), choline for neurological diseases and aging (US Patent #4,737,489) or for enhancing muscular performance (US Patent #4,626,527), and L-tryptophan for increasing brain serotonin levels (US Patent #4,687,763) or for reducing depression (US Patent #4,377,595).

This is the ultimate in hypocrisy: Wurtman states that all amino acids are toxic and should be taken off the OTC market; all the while he is secretly accumulating use permits so that when amino acids are removed (as appears imminent), he is ready to roll.

The problem with use patents, from the patent-holder's point of view, is that they are only salable *if the nutrient in question cannot be purchased OTC.* This is the rub, and probably explains Wurtman's testimony before a House Subcommittee Hearing last year where he implored Congress to ban OTC sales of amino acids. I particularly enjoyed his statement to the effect that "L-tryptophan has nothing to do with nutrition." This comment is rather inane considering the essential nature of this amino acid in human nutrition.

Unfortunately, Wurtman is not alone in his greed, and there seems to be a trend towards profiteering at the expense of the nation's health. Dr. Stephen De Felice, for example, has long been trying to get carnitine removed from the OTC market, as his patents can't be sold to drug companies (e.g., Sigma Tau, which already markets a "drug" form of carnitine called Carnitor®— actually nothing more than L-carnitine at many-fold the OTC price) until this is accomplished. I met De Felice in 1983 just prior to publication of my book on carnitine; I still remember him telling me what a great drug carnitine could be. De Felice's latest thing is "nutraceuticals"— nutrients turned into pharmaceuticals. A recent paper describes De Felice's "Nutraceutical Initiative: A Proposal for Economic and Regulatory Reform":

> *"A nutraceutical can be defined as any substance that may be considered a food or part of a food that provides medical or health benefits, including the prevention and treatment of disease. Nutraceuticals may range from*

isolated nutrients, dietary supplements, and diets to genetically engineered 'designer' foods, herbal products, and processed products, such as cereals, soups, and beverages."[18]

Apparently, De Felice won't be satisfied with just getting carnitine classed as a drug; he wants it all — vitamins, minerals, non-vitamin nutrients, herbs, foods, etc. I believe that De Felice has similar goals, namely, the use of nutrients for preventing and treating diseases; the only difference is that he wants to make his fortune selling us the nutrients at manyfold their OTC price.

There are, of course, a number of easier ways to make a nutrient into a drug. You can oxidize it (retinoids), add a chlorine or two (4',6-dichloroflavan), methyoxylate it (gluta-thione monomethylester), dimerize it (sodium cromolyn) or acetylate it (acetyl-L-carnitine). You can even link it to another vitamin, as in Juvela-Nicotinate® (dl-alpha tocopherol nico-tinate) — or a non-vitamin nutrient, as in Hexopal (inositol nicotinate).

Complicity in the Nutrition Community

This is perhaps the most difficult aspect to comprehend — why those at the very top levels of nutrition tacitly, and some-times not so tacitly, accept the dogma about supplements being worthless. Dr. Victor Herbert, a Professor of medicine at Mount Sinai School of Medicine, is the best example of how nutritionists assist the FDA and others in suppressing the use of nutritional supplements.

This is exemplified in an article by Victor Herbert appearing in the March/April issue of *Nutrition Today* (not peer-reviewed, despite Victor's criticism of such journals).[19] Victor has really outdone himself in this article which, in my opinion, is not even a reasonable facsimile of science. It certainly ranks among his worst, and that's saying quite a bit as Victor has penned some real dillies. Remember the fable about vitamin C destroying vitamin B_{12} in foods? That was one of Victor's contributions to nutrition science. [Note: some text-books, even today, still use B_{12} destruction as a "toxic effect" of vitamin C, even though it's been unequivocally disproved. The error, as it turned out, was that Victor used the wrong assay for vitamin B_{12}.]

Victor's "Medicolegal" Case Against OTC Aminos. There are so many errors that we'll only be able to mention a few of the more important ones. Victor stated that, "The potential toxicity of large doses of single amino acids led the FDA to remove these from the GRAS [generally recognized as safe] list in 1974." *But where is the evidence of individual amino acid toxicity when given as oral supplements?* Aside from EMS (a disease which was due to a contaminant in L-tryptophan supplements), his one reference to a peer-reviewed journal was a 1958 study by Fahey in which *intravenous* amino acids raised blood ammonia. His only other "reference" to amino acid toxicity is a book by none other than Richard Wurtman.

If amino acid toxicity was as well known as Victor implied, there must be some references in the literature. Why aren't more references cited by Herbert regarding amino acid toxicity? It's simple: there's virtually nothing to cite. Amino acids are not toxic despite proclamations by Victor Herbert, Richard Wurtman, or the FDA.

Although a number of false "toxic effects" were mentioned (like the unreferenced accusation that "large doses of L-tryptophan will block gluconeogenesis" [new glucose synthesis]), Victor missed the only real undesirable side-effect of aminos (diarrhea at very high intakes, as occurs with consumption of large amounts of any substance). Victor has consistently criticized the supplement industry for unsubstantiated claims; well, where is his proof? In his summary, Victor states that:

> *"Not only is there no need for free tryptophan in the diet, but free tryptophan is not recognized as safe by the Food and Drug Administration. It is a drug whose only use is as a drug or food additive (in infant formulas, medical foods, and as an additive to tryptophan-poor protein of plant origin)."* [19]

Without getting into the specifics of this moronic statement, I'd just like to know why, if free tryptophan is not recognized as safe by the FDA, is it being fed to babies and given to people as a drug?

Stonewalling in Academia. I have observed an incredible resistance to the *Journal of Optimal Nutrition* at the very top of the academic community. Both the *American Journal of Clinical Nutrition* and the *Journal of Nutrition* refused to run my "call for papers" notice (a paid advertisement). This is in spite of the fact that they had run *the exact same ad* for three and six months, respectively, the previous year (when I was Editor-in-Chief of *The Journal of Applied Nutrition*). [In truth, the ads were slightly different: *The Journal of* Applied *Nutrition* was changed to *The Journal of* Optimal *Nutrition*].

Neither *AJCN* nor *JN* responded in writing to my written requests, nor were any reasons given for their rejections. Even more lamentable was that I was not told how to change the ad to make it acceptable. All I got from *JN* was the proverbial run-around, and all I was told was that "someone had said they didn't like it." I tried, in vain, to find out more about how they had arrived at their decision by contacting Dr. Willard Visek (the Editor-in-Chief of *JN*). The irony was that I had been elected to the American Institute of Nutrition (*JN*'s parent organization) the same week as the rejection occurred. Nice welcome!

The story at *AJCN* was much the same: Dr. Stephen Schiaffino, the Managing Editor of *AJCN*, said that he'd asked *four* individuals about this ad, and they all disapproved. When asked how many he had to choose from, his response was "five hundred," but on further questioning he was unwilling to get any other opinions. In essence, I was told that 0.8% of the total reviewing board was sufficient to reject the *JON* 'call for papers' ad. Further discussions with Dr. Norman Kretchmer (Editor-in-Chief of *AJCN*) were equally revealing. He told me that *AJCN* didn't have to say why the ad was rejected, or let me know how it could be changed to make it acceptable, or even respond in writing!

One take-home lesson is that there is something amiss with the decision-making process at the very highest echelons of academic nutrition — levels I'd previously thought immune to petty politics and common corruption.

The Bottom Line: Fear. I also brought this up to illustrate the depth of resistance to any one or any group focusing on the *science of nutritional supplements.* I definitely got the impression that there was no clear way either *JN* or *AJCN* would carry the ad, not because of me personally, but because of what *JON* represents. But of greater import is the fear that gets registered every time the terms "science" and "supplements" are used in the same sentence.

Nutritionists are terrified of even appearing to be supplement-oriented, fearing (probably rightfully so) that their grants would be cut and their reputations ruined. At several free radical/antioxidant meetings, I have proposed that we (the leaders in antioxidant research) make some recommendations to the general public, as we have the knowledge (and responsibility) to do so. No recommendations ever emerged, however; the fear was simply too great. Moreover, several members of *JON*'s Editorial Board have related instances where they have been warned *not* to publish positive results on supplemental nutrients, for by doing so their careers would suffer.

The fear of having one's career ruined is, in my estimation, one of the methods whereby the system has survived for so many years. It is this same system which promotes the use of the wrong medicines — ones which at best are ineffective, at worst, lethal. It is the same system which brings you the PDCAAS, the RDI, and genetically recombined vegetables.

I believe that as nutritionists we can no longer hide behind the veil of academia; we must stand up for what we know to be the truth. If not, we are guilty of complicity with a deplorable system of medicine.

The (Oyster) Shell Game

The health food industry has its own problems, including ones of honesty and integrity. One example is a multi-mineral supplement we'll call "Brand X." The label claimed that two tablets contained the following amounts of *elemental* minerals: 1,000 mg of calcium; 500 mg of magnesium; 99 mg of potassium; and about 100 mg of other minerals. In total, Brand X claimed to have about 1.7 grams of elemental minerals in two tablets with a total weight of 4.8 grams. According to the label, they were in the form of amino acid and organic acid chelates.

Mineral chelates, however, contain only 10-25% of the elemental mineral (on a weight basis). For example, calcium citrate is only 24% calcium, calcium lactate only 18% calcium, and calcium gluconate only 9% elemental calcium.

If all of Brand X's calcium were actually in the form of calcium citrate (with the highest percentage of calcium), the weight of 1 gram of elemental calcium would be a minimum of 4 grams. The total weight of their 1.7 grams of elemental minerals would be at least 6.8 grams. And that's giving them the benefit of the doubt by using citrate as the chelator.

False label claims like these damage the industry's credibility, and underscore the need for quality control in the health food industry. There's no reason why nutrient supplements cannot be prepared using the same meticulous standards used by pharmaceutical companies. The industry as a group needs to set such standards and, more importantly, enforce them.

You Get All You Need from a Well-Balanced Diet

"If you eat a variety of foods from among and within the Basic Four Food Groups and adjust portion size, particularly of those foods generous in fats, to reach and maintain a reasonable weight, you will be as well nourished as your genetic potential permits." [20]

This statement is from Dr. Frederick Stare, but it could have come from anyone. This concept is so well entrenched that no one questions its validity anymore. This is dogma as ingrained as that which once decreed that the world is flat. Yes, the diet provides all one needs for preventing nutritional deficiencies, that is, for *adequate* health.

But that's as far as it goes. There is not a *shred of evidence* that diet alone can supply enough micronutrients to attain any level of health above adequate. I've never seen a single study to support the concept that you get everything you need for optimal health from a well-balanced diet. This is due, in part, to our asking the wrong questions. Instead of nutrient deficiencies, as we've studied for so long — and as many nutritionists still study — we need to focus on supplemental nutrients, for only through supplemental nutrients can we achieve optimal health.

For it is my belief that nature, which wants us to reproduce and then die, ensures these events by limiting the number of micronutrients which may be obtained from our caloric intake. If one ate lemons all day, one might be optimal in vitamin C, bioflavonoids, and possibly terpenes, but deficient in everything else. And for the first time in mankind's history, we now have the knowledge and capabilities to extract these wondrous factors from foodstuffs, and ingest them in sufficient quantities to achieve a state of optimal health.

References

1. Packer M, Carver JR, Rodeheffer RJ, et al. Effect of oral milrinone on mortality in severe chronic heart failure. N Engl J Med 325: 1468-75, 1991.
2. The National Cholesterol Education Program Expert Panel. Report on detection, evaluation, and treatment of high blood cholesterol in adults. Arch Int Med 148: 36-69, 1988.
3. Marshall E. Artificial heart: The beat goes on. Science 253: 500-02, 1991.
4. Bodey G. Infections in cancer patients. Cancer Treatment Rev 2: 89-128, 1975.
5. Penn I. Review of "Cancer risk after medical treatment," Coleman M (ed), Oxford University Press, NY, 1991. This review appeared in N Engl J Med 326: 1298-99, 1992.
6. Muss HB, Case LD, Richards F. Interrupted versus continuous chemotherapy in patients with metastatic breast cancer. N Engl J Med 325: 1342-48, 1991.
7. Olson R, Boerth R, Gerber J, et al. Mini-review: mechanism of adriamycin cardiotoxicity: Evidence for oxidative stress. Life Sci 29: 1393-1401, 1982.
8. Marshall E. Breast cancer: Stalemate in the war on cancer. Science 254: 1719-20, 1991.
9. Ingram B. Cancer strides challenged: Establishment's therapeutic claims overstated, says activist coalition. Medical Tribune 33: 1, 1992.
10. Stepp W, Kuhnau D, Schroeder H. The vitamins and their clinical applications. The Vitamin Products, Co., Milwaukee, WI, pg. xiii, 1938.
11. Toufexis A. The new scoop on vitamins. Time 139(14): 54-9, 1992.
12. Slutsker L, Hoesly F, Miller L, et al. Eosinophilia-myalgia syndrome associated with exposure to tryptophan from a single manufacturer. JAMA 264: 213-7, 1990.
13. Sakimoto K. The cause of the eosinophilia-myalgia syndrome associated with tryptophan use. N Engl J Med 323: 992-3, 1990.
14. Mayeno A, Lin F, Foote C, et al. Characterization of "peak E," a novel

amino acid associated with eosinophilia myalgia syndrome. *Science* 250: 1707-8, 1990.

15. Raphals P. Disease puzzle nears solution. *Science* 249: 619, 1990.
16. Beelongia E, Hedberg C, Gleich G, *et al.* An investigation of the cause of the eosinophilia myalgia syndrome associated with tryptophan use. *N Engl J Med* 323: 357-65, 1990.
17. Henley EC. Food and Drug Administration's proposed labeling rules for protein. *J Am Dietics Assoc* 92: 293-96, 1990.
18. Psczcola DE. The nutraceutical initiative: A proposal for economic and regulatory reform. *Food Tech* (April): 77-79, 1992.
19. Herbert V. L-tryptophan. A medicolegal case against over-the-counter marketing of supplements of amino acids. *Nutr Today* (March/April): 27-30, 1992.
20. Stare F. Some more comments on Silent Spring. *Nutr Rev* 50: 61-2, 1992.

Editor's Note: *This article is copyright © 1992 by the Institute for the Study of Optimal Nutrition, originally published in* The Journal of Optimal Nutrition *1(1): 69-83, 1992. Reprinted with permission.* JON *is a quarterly peer-reviewed journal which focuses on supplementary micronutrients (vitamins, minerals, non-vitamin nutrients, etc.) and macronutrients (carbohydrates, lipids, proteins, etc.) in the prevention and treatment of disease, as well as the maintenance of optimal health. For membership in ISON and subscription to* JON, *write to: JON Subscription Department, 2552 Regis Drive, Davis, CA 95616. Annual memberships are $75/year (in the US), $90/year (foreign). Special membership rates for students are $25/year (in the US) and $40/year (foreign). Please include your name, address, phone number, date, and profession along with your membership check. Phone: 916-756-3311. FAX: 916- 758-7444.*

Back-in-Action Jackson

by Terry Jackson

Terry Jackson is a stuntman who lives and works in Hollywood, California. He has appeared in such shows as Hunter *and* LA Law, *and such movies as* Red Dawn, Back to the Future, Who Framed Roger Rabbit *and* Terminator 2. *His wife, Donna Evans, is an award-winning stuntwoman. She was the one in the knock-down drag-out fight with Arnold Schwartzneger in* Total Recall. *The Jacksons are definitely an action-packed family.*

As a professional stuntman, I earn my living jumping off of buildings, crashing cars, sliding motorcycles, and rolling car-carrier trucks. When I was 14, I decided to be a stuntman. I started jumping off of buildings into cardboard boxes, and by the time I was 17 I was leaping off seven-story buildings.

My first big break was the film *Red Dawn* directed by John Milius. Then five years of stuntwork for *Hunter* established me in the industry. During my first year, I performed an award-winning stunt where I laid a motorcycle down and slid under a tractor-trailer turning in front of me at 55 miles per hour. In the dozen years since, I have done more than a hundred stunts for such films and shows as *Cheers, Matlock, LA Law, Terminator 2, Hot Shots, Dragnet* (doubling Tom Hanks), *Who Framed Roger Rabbit, Farewell to the King* (doubling Nick Nolte), *Cobra, The Rookie* (doubling Clint Eastwood), *Back to the Future*, and all of John Milius' films since *Red Dawn*.

After 13 years of hard work, I had established a reputation as a reliable, hard-working and skilled stuntman. While working on *RoboCop III*, I went to work on a pilot for a new series for Universal TV called *Robosaurus*.

The Fall

The stunt called for me to fly through the air from one tall building to another. Since I had only five steps to work with before the edge of the building, we decided to use an air ram, a device for using compressed air to launch me over the chasm between the buildings. I was ready, but the air ram failed. Instead of shooting over the gap between two buildings, I fell between them. Bouncing off the wall of the far building, I severely sprained my right foot and brutally smashed my left foot. Ricocheting off the near building, I fractured my skull. The resulting cerebral hematoma and bruising of my brain left me delirious. I wanted to get up and do the stunt again, but I ended up in the hospital with multiple serious injuries, contemplating the end of my career.

In the hospital, they rebuilt my left foot with multiple steel pins and a bone graft from my hip to reconstruct my shattered heel. After three weeks in the hospital flat on my back, I was finally allowed up on crutches. When the cast came off, I was faced with learning to walk. After so many weeks of inactivity, my well-sculpted, bicycle-conditioned leg muscles had atrophied to nothing. Walking was not only intensely painful, it was almost impossible.

Three months after the accident, I was able to hobble painfully without crutches for short periods after intense physical therapy sessions. Then I met screenwriter Kirk Sullivan, and, after a lengthy conversation, decided to augment my mental determination to recover with a special nutrient supplement program. To enhance my healing, I started with Power Maker II, a Pearson & Shaw formulation containing lots of the amino acid arginine. Just three weeks later, I was back at work doing a back-fall off a balcony onto a break-away table — and I've been working ever since.

Adding nutrient supplements to my professional fitness program made all the difference in my being able to reestablish my professional credibility. Without them, my career probably would have been over. With them, I am not only back at work doing what I love to do, I am physically stronger, fitter, and faster than I was before the accident. It is not only my physical condition which has improved. I now have more mental energy and stamina for the 10-14 hour days typically required for top stuntmen. I do far more now in a day than I did two years ago.

New Views of Nutrition

Although I had used vitamins on and off for years earlier, it took an accident to make the real value of nutrients apparent to me in a way that changed my life. I now know, rationally and emotionally, that vitamins saved my life, and my dream of being a stuntman. People close to me, my wife and professional colleagues, have shared in my discovery and have also come to appreciate the value of nutrition. However, not all see it as I do. My miraculous recovery has some people discounting the seriousness of the original accident. If I didn't have the accident on film, from multiple angles, nobody seeing me now would believe what had happened to me.

The medical professionals working on my case were universally surprised by my recovery, but they have no experience or training with the nutrition techniques I used. Not one of them had heard of arginine-assisted healing, even though I have now read dozens of scientific papers reporting on such effects dating back decades.

Now I hear that the FDA wants to ban all amino acids, including those that helped me. I think they probably believe that they are doing this to protect me and the rest of the public, but I don't want their protection, and I don't need their protection. I sincerely hope that the original vision of our founding fathers — freedom — survives their sadly misguided paternalistic efforts.

Given a choice, I would no more do without nutrient supplements than I would food, exercise, water or air. I hope that other Americans will continue to have the same opportunities to utilize nutrition in their lives that I had.

Vitamin C: The Key to Health

by Linus Pauling, PhD — a speech
given to the Schizophrenia Foundation

"The ethical principle of minimizing human suffering requires we all work together in overcoming the causes of suffering."   — Linus Pauling, 1962

Introduction by Dr. Abram Hoffer, MD, PhD

In the world of science and medicine, Linus Pauling stands preeminent. There has never been a scientist with his stature, with his great contributions to humanity, and whose discoveries have less lent themselves to abuse. What has driven this brilliant scientist to continue his never-ending quest to better humanity against the carping and the criticism of the medical profession? I was curious until I read a statement he made in 1962. He said, "The ethical principle of minimizing human suffering requires we all work together in overcoming the causes of suffering. I believe the time will come, perhaps in 10 or 20 years, when — if enough effort is made — there will be obtained some understanding of the nature of the group of diseases we classify as schizophrenia, and of other mental diseases comparable to that which now exists for a few diseases that are called 'molecular diseases.'"

Professor Linus Pauling has been motivated by his personal ethics — that is, to help humanity lessen its suffering. Dr. Pauling's work falls into three main phases. His earliest was a strictly chemical phase when he discovered the laws which describe how molecules interact with each other. These laws which describe how molecules interact have been of enormous importance to medical and biochemical research. Modern medicine would have been entirely different if Linus Pauling had not done his work. The second phase of his work was in the anti-radiation and peace movement. Dr. Pauling enjoyed his chemical research so much he did not think he should have gotten a Nobel Prize — that is, for doing something he found so pleasant. His public campaign against atomic-bomb testing and against radiation he found very difficult and not enjoyable. Only his strong ethic kept him going. When he got his second Nobel for this, he felt this time he deserved it, but it probably cost him the third Nobel. The American government seized his passport and he was unable to attend a meeting in England which provided the final clue he needed, in addition to the work he had done, to propose the double helix as the basic unit of the long-chain protein molecules in the chromosomes.

His third phase began when he was 65 when, instead of retiring, he became interested in the relationship between nutrition and the use of large doses of vitamins in the treatment of diseases. This is the "orthomolecular" phase, a term he proposed in his classic paper in *Science* in 1968. The ortho-molecular phase may be divided into three: (1) his finding that there was enough material in the medical literature to conclude that vitamin C would be helpful in dealing with the cold and then flu; (2) his discovery that vitamin C in very large doses would be therapeutic for cancer; and (3) his most recent phase, his conclusion that vitamin C plays a decisive role in the preven-tion of arteriosclerosis. You will read more about this later.

I consider Linus Pauling to be a great physician. Not one who treats people, for he has no medical license, but a teacher who has made it possible for thousands of physicians to treat their patients better and more successfully. If I had any influence, I would recommend that the University of Toronto Medical School award him an honorary medical degree. He already has plenty of doctorates in science and philosophy from grateful universities. Ladies and gentlemen, please join me in welcoming Professor Linus Pauling.

Dr. Pauling's Speech

Some 25 years ago, when I first became interested in vita-mins (vitamin C and other vitamins), I read that if somebody says that he knows something that is good for you no matter what's wrong with you, then he's a quack. So very soon I was saying, "Well I guess I'm a quack because I know something that's good for you no matter what's wrong with you, and that is vitamin C." The reason that I can say that is that nearly every-one on earth is suffering from a disease which Irwin Stone called "hypovitaminosis," or hypovitaminosis-C — I guess he called it "hypoascorbemia," having too little vitamin C (ascorbic acid) in the blood. The result of this is poor health.

Every person on earth is essentially in poor health. It's called "ordinary good health," but it ought to be called "ordinary poor health." And because of this small amount of vitamin C in the blood, and because vitamin C is involved in so many of the body's protective mechanisms, we are poorly protected against ravages by disease — diseases of all kinds. To be in true good health requires much more vitamin C than people get in their food — much more than the RDA, which in the United States is 60 mg a day for an adult. Because of the low intake of vitamin C, people suffer much more from the onslaught of disease, people have a shorter period of good health, and people die earlier than they should.

I myself am now taking 300 times the RDA of vitamin C. I began 25 years ago taking 50 times the RDA. I had been taking ordinary vitamin pills for many years already, since 1941, but when I went up to 50 times the 60 mg RDA of vitamin C, I felt better. After some years I went up to 100 times (6 grams), and then to 200 times, and then to 300 times the RDA.

I think I should tell about how I got to the point of being interested in the vitamins and being here tonight. I believe that this is going to be perhaps the greatest day in my life, the one that I look back on with the most satisfaction, and I'm glad that it is here that I am experiencing this particular period in my life, one about which I am extremely enthusiastic. The history, the reason, the way that I got this way, where I am now, is that I gave a lecture in New York in 1965. A biochemist in the audience wrote to me about something that I had said, "I enjoy so much learning more about the nature of the universe, reading about what scientists have discovered, things that they have dis-covered about the nature of the universe, that I hope that I can continue to have this pleasure for another 25 years." The writer was Irwin Stone, and he wrote saying that he was sending me some papers that he had written and, if I followed his recommendation to take 3,000 mg of vitamin C a day instead of 60 mg a day, I would be able to live not just 25 years but 50 years longer. So I began taking the 3,000 mg a day. His arguments were so logical, it seemed to me that I couldn't help but believe that there was something to what he said.

I didn't have any intention of getting heavily involved in the vitamin field, except that I became interested in my own health and what vitamins might do for me. But then it happened that I came across the work of Abram Hoffer and Humphrey Osmond. I had been working for ten years on the molecular basis of mental disease when I read what Hoffer and Osmond had done in Saskatchewan, giving vitamin B_3 (niacin) to schizo-phrenic patients — and also ascorbic acid (vitamin C). At first it didn't make a very great impression on me. I just didn't know much about vitamins.

After perhaps a week, I thought, "There is something odd here. Here I am 66 years old and I've never heard of substances like these vitamins having the properties these vitamins had." The point was we know that a little pinch — a few milligrams of vitamin C a day — is enough to keep people from dying of scurvy. A little pinch of nicotinic acid (niacin) is enough to keep people from dying of pellagra. But Hoffer and Osmond were giving a thousand times or ten thousand times these amounts, and they had powerful physiological effects other than keeping people from dying.

Well, I knew a moderate amount about drugs, and I knew that a drug that has some effectiveness against a disease is more effective the larger the amount that you give. So I knew that doctors, in being very sensible people, and the medical profes-sion, having studied these problems for a long time, felt that if a person is seriously ill and there is a possibility of saving his or her life by use of the drug, then you should give as much of the drug as you can in order to increase the probability of saving the person's life. And the upper limit is that if you give too much of a drug, you hurt or kill the person. So you have to compromise by giving somewhat less than the toxic or lethal dose, and this is what physicians do.

What about the vitamins? Here are these extraordinary

substances that have very powerful physiological effects when they are given in small amounts to people, enough to keep people alive. And yet there is a range of a thousandfold or ten thousandfold in intakes over which these substances can be taken without killing the person. And I thought, "There are two questions that we might ask about a vitamin." First, how much does a person need in order not to die of the corresponding deficiency disease? We know the answer to that. That's the RDA, the Recommended Dietary Allowances set by the appropriate government or semi-governmental bodies. The RDAs are enough to keep people barely alive in ordinary poor health.

The other question is, over this great possible range of intakes, where is the intake that puts people in the best of health? As a scientist, I thought, "Well, I'd better look in the literature and find out what the answers to this question are for different vitamins." And I thought, "It's astonishing that I haven't read about the optimum intakes of vitamins in the 63 years that I've been reading." When I looked in the literature, I couldn't find anything. So I thought, "It's odder still that this important question hasn't been answered." The result, of course, is that for the last 25 years I've spent a large amount of time and energy trying to answer it.

So Hoffer and Osmond are important to me. The first paper I wrote in the field was the paper "Orthomolecular Psychiatry." There was another one, "Orthomolecular Psychiatric and Somatic Medicine," that I published in 1968, introducing the word "orthomolecular" (equivalent in a sense to "megavitamins," but a larger class including all substances normally present in the human body). I thought that would be the end of it. It was a good logical paper with a number of new ideas in it, one of them being that if an animal manufactures a vital substance for itself, it can still benefit by being given an additional amount of that vital substance.

I shan't repeat the argument that led me to that conclusion in detail, but simply, as an example: dogs and cats make their own vitamin C, but if they are sick they benefit a lot by receiving additional vitamin C.

Although I thought that was the end, I was asked to give a talk at the dedication of a new medical school and I thought, "I must say something *medical*." What do I know? Well, I know that since I've been taking 3 grams of vitamin C a day, I don't catch colds. So I'll say that you can control the common cold, to some extent at any rate, by taking 3 grams of vitamin C a day. I got a letter from a professor of medicine just 'giving me the devil' for having made that statement and asking could I point to any evidence in the literature. Well, I found four good papers describing double-blind randomized studies that showed that vitamin C had value, but he wouldn't pay any attention to these papers.

I was irritated enough by his reaction to look through the literature and what I found interested me enough that I sat down and wrote my book, *Vitamin C and the Common Cold*, and a later edition, *Vitamin C, the Common Cold and the Flu*, and then a book with Ewan Cameron, *Cancer and Vitamin C*, and finally the book *How to Live Longer and Feel Better*. I began carrying out research on this whole question of how much should be the intake of various vitamins and other natural orthomolecular substances to put people in the best of health.

What are the principal arguments about vitamin C? First, why is it that all plants manufacture vitamins that animals require? Vitamin A, vitamin E, vitamin B_1, vitamin B_2 and so on; animals require them, plants don't. Plants and animals are pretty closely similar; their biochemistry is nearly the same — remarkable similarities not only in the reactions that go on but in the structures of molecules. Plants, of course, have some special molecules for photosynthesis and animals have some special molecules, too, but otherwise they are remarkably similar.

The answer, I think, is that when the first animal began running around and eating its plant relatives, its biochemistry was about the same. It was getting the vitamins that plants manufactured. It was getting these vitamins from its food. It was burdened by having machinery for making them, so when mutations occurred discarding this machinery, the mutant benefited by not being burdened with useless biochemical machinery. Irwin Stone pointed out, and others had too, that vitamin C is an exception. Animals in general did not abandon the manufacture of vitamin C. They have kept on manufacturing it. Ninety-nine-point-nine percent of all animals (or 99.99% perhaps) manufacture ascorbic acid — *they don't require it as a vitamin*! They aren't satisfied with what they get in their food.

Why? Why would they continue to manufacture vitamin C unless it makes them healthier to manufacture more than they get in their food? Surely the reason that they continue to make it is that larger amounts of vitamin C are valuable to them. I thought, a goat weighing 150 pounds (the size of a man) manufactures 13 grams of vitamin C a day, about 200 times the RDA for a human being of that size. Why shouldn't the goat, after generations of goats, be satisfied to manufacture 12 grams rather than 13 grams and save 8% of the energy and materials? The answer must be that the 13th gram has value for the goat.

So what happened to human beings? We can make a good surmise as to why human beings are the exception — one of the *few* exceptions. An ancestor of the human being, living in a tropical valley, eating high-vitamin C fruits and vegetables, was getting so much vitamin C that when the mutant came along that had lost the ability to synthesize vitamin C, that mutant had an advantage over the wild type. And as a result, the wild type of this ancestor died out and the mutant remained. We can estimate that this occurred 40 million years ago. This is based on established fact. The dog, the cat, the cow, the horse, the elephant and so on all manufacture vitamin C. But human beings, the anthropoid apes, and the monkeys — the primates as a whole — lost the ability to make vitamin C.

So presumably, the common ancestor to all primates had a bad accident that makes all human beings suffer with poor health rather than the good health that they would have without the vitamin C mutation or living in a vitamin C-rich environment. A similar accident happened to the guinea pig, another animal that requires vitamin C in its diet.

So vitamin C is an exception among the vitamins. From these arguments we can conclude that the amount of vitamin C that human beings ought to be getting could be quite large. How large? If you study animals you find that they manufacture vitamin C in amounts roughly proportional to body weight. About 10 to 12 grams for 150 pounds of animal. This amount is pretty constant, whether we speak of houseflies or elephants, it's usually about 10 or 12 grams a day per 150 pounds. By this argument, instead of 60 mg a day, we ought to be taking 200 times that much — 12,000 mg a day — to be in the sort of good health that other animals are in.

There is another argument, too, provided by the committee on the care of laboratory animals, the animals used in laboratory studies of disease processes, health, and so on. It's very important that these laboratory animals (monkeys, guinea pigs, mice, rats, dogs, and so on) be in good health. So people have studied the diets of these animals to see what puts them in the best of health. Well, the chow for mice and rats doesn't contain any added vitamin C; it contains all the other vitamins. The chow for monkeys has to have added vitamin C because ascorbate is a vitamin for monkeys just as it is for men. And this committee recommends 50 times as much vitamin C for monkeys as the Food and Nutrition Board recommends for human beings. And they recommend similarly for guinea pigs, 50 times as much vitamin C in guinea pig chow to keep the guinea pigs in the best of health as the amount that corresponds to the human RDA. There has never been any committee that has studied human beings to find this same optimum intake, but I am sure that it is somewhere in the range of a thousand or ten thousand or perhaps eighteen thousand milligrams a day, not 60 mg a day.

For the other vitamins, there is also information that an increased intake does a lot of good. The literature is full of this information about the different vitamins. Here we have the Shute Institute, Evan Shute and Wilfred Shute, giving a thousand times or two thousand times the RDA of vitamin E to patients with heart disease with remarkable results. I've been taking 80 times the RDA of vitamin E for a long time. The B vitamins also have considerable evidence about the value of additional intake. I've been taking a super B tablet that contains 25 times the RDA of various B vitamins, and I also take beta-carotene to get additional vitamin A. The amounts that I take correspond to my conclusions as to what the optimum intakes of these most important substances are.

All of this explains why, in my book *How To Live Longer and Feel Better* I say that following a regimen of very high intake of vitamin C, high intakes of other vitamins, and good intakes of essential minerals, one can be in really good health rather than in ordinary poor health. I may discuss a hundred diseases in my book, and certainly Irwin Stone does in his book *The Healing Factor: Vitamin C Against Disease* published in 1972, where vitamin C plays an important role in helping to control it, and where there were references in the literature about clinical reports of the value of increased vitamin C intake in controlling about 100 diseases.

I remember when Abram Hoffer wrote a letter to *The New England Journal of Medicine* complaining about treatment of me by physicians. He said in his letter, "Critics of Dr. Pauling require of him the most rigorous sort of controlled double-blind prospective clinical study to support his statements, but they are willing to criticize him on the flimsiest of information." This is true. For example, half an hour ago someone said to me, "My doctor says you shouldn't take high-dose vitamin C because it causes kidney stones." And I said, "Well it just isn't true. It doesn't cause kidney stones." This is the sort of misinformation which is rampant among physicians. They haven't read the literature. They get their information mainly by talking with other physicians at meetings, or perhaps from the authorities.

My criticism is not really directed against physicians. They're doing valuable work, and hard work, too. I feel it's probably not too pleasant a life. Physicians have a lot of responsibility, they have to work long hours, and they don't have time to read the literature personally, to think, analyze, and make up their own minds. It's inevitable that physicians rely on the authorities. Really, it's the medical authorities that I am criticizing. I say they're lazy and incompetent. They don't try to keep up with the advance of knowledge. They're biased and they are not attempting to improve medical practice in the way that they should.

What happened next was that I was asked to speak at the opening ceremony at a new laboratory for cancer research. I thought, "Well, I must say something about *cancer*." While I was checking the literature on vitamin C in relation to the common cold, I kept running across reports on vitamin C in relation to cancer. I read a good number of these papers and, when I gave my talk (a short one at this dedication ceremony) I said that on the basis of the information that I had gathered by reading the literature and some general scientific considerations, I believed that it would be possible to decrease the incidence of mortality from cancer by 10 percent by the proper use of vitamin C.

Well, I've been changing my estimate every few years since then; decrease by 25 percent, 50 percent, 75 percent or more. Dr. Cameron gave 10 grams a day of vitamin C to his patients with essentially terminal cancer. Measured from the date when the patient was declared to be untreatable, he found that the vitamin C patients receiving 10 grams a day lived several times as long as similar patients who did not receive the vitamin C — perhaps six times as long. Instead of living four months (median time), they would live two years or more (median time).

Then Abram Hoffer asked me if I were interested in his observations on patients who had come to him for psychiatric treatment but who also had cancer. The treatment that he gave them to help control the psychiatric problems seemed to be helping to control their cancers as well. The results that he was getting were even better than Ewan Cameron's results. A quarter of the patients who came to him refused to follow his regimen of (usually) 12 grams of vitamin C per day, plus — and here it differed from Cameron — plus 500-800 IUs of vitamin E, 1.5 to 2.5 grams a day of B_3, and good amounts of other vitamins, selenium, and perhaps some other minerals. On average, his patients who *followed* his regimen, measured from the date when they had been referred to him, lived 16 times as long as the ones who did *not* follow the regimen. Some didn't follow the regimen because doctors said, "You shouldn't take all those vitamins, it'll kill you." So they didn't. Others perhaps were upset by taking the vitamins, a stomach upset or something like that, and decided not to do it.

It looks as though not only high doses of vitamin C (usually 12 grams per day) but also the other nutrients have considerable value in controlling advanced cancer. Also, during the last three years, there has been increased interest in the evidence about the value of foods that are high in vitamin C, vitamin E and vitamin A for decreasing the incidence of, and mortality from, cancer and other diseases.

In my book published six years ago, *How To Live Longer and Feel Better*, there was a chapter on heart disease. I quoted some information about the high intake of vitamin C and heart disease, but at that time I didn't know what the most significant arguments were. In fact, they hadn't been discovered yet. So now I can talk about cardiovascular disease and stroke. Cancer is the cause of about 20 percent of deaths in the United States, but heart disease and stroke are the cause of 50 percent of deaths, a million deaths a year, and the cause of a great amount of disability. Throughout the world, perhaps 12 million people a year die of cardiovascular disease, heart disease and strokes. It's a very serious medical health problem.

About ten years ago, I became acquainted with a young medical student and kept up the acquaintance for years. I encouraged him to work harder, to get his MD degree, and to think about doing medical research. I've seen him often during the ten years, but three years ago he came to California to talk with me. He had been working in Hamburg and Berlin, and had decided to follow up the investigations he was carrying out by moving to the United States.

When I asked what he had been doing after he got his MD degree, he said he had been doing medical research on atherosclerosis. He was the principal investigator of a study published three years ago in which he and his colleagues took specimens of aorta from 107 patients with cardiovascular disease who had bypass operations and examined the atherosclerotic plaques on the arterial walls of these samples. They checked the atherosclerotic plaques by applying two kinds of antibodies that reacted with the atherosclerotic plaques: antibodies against

LDL apoprotein, the protein part of the ordinary low-density lipoprotein, and against apoprotein-a. The amount of the antibody against the LDL apoprotein was just equal to the amount against apoprotein-a. But lipoprotein-a has a protein that consists of both the LDL apoprotein and apoprotein-a. Accordingly, Dr. Rath and his collaborators had made the important discovery that the plaques consist solely of lipoprotein-a.

There are several lipoproteins in the blood. LDL is the one present in the largest amounts and is usually the one reported when you have a blood analysis for cholesterol. To make lipoprotein-a, you add another piece of protein and put some more cholesterol inside the globule. Altogether, the amount of lipoprotein-a is considerably smaller than the amount of LDL. The main function of LDL is to carry cholesterol from the liver, where it's manufactured, to the cells throughout the body.

There is another protein, called high-density lipoprotein (HDL), that picks up cholesterol and carries it back to the liver to be destroyed. It is said that people are in better health the smaller the amount of LDL they have and the larger the amount of high-density HDL they have. HDL cuts down the amount of cholesterol that might be deposited in atherosclerotic plaques.

It turns out, because of the discovery of Dr. Rath and his associates, that LDL itself is not the culprit. It is this other minor constituent of blood, lipoprotein-a, that is laid down in atherosclerotic plaques. Their evidence indicates that the antibody against the LDL and the antibody against the additional lipoprotein-a are attached to these plaques *in equal amounts*. There isn't an excess of the anti-LDL antibody. I think it's generally accepted that this conclusion is correct. This minor constituent of the blood (lipoprotein-a), that doctors usually ignore and that laboratories don't usually have the means of measuring, is the real culprit.

I can give you some more information about lipoprotein-a. Lipoprotein-a differs from many other bodily constituents in that the range of values for different human beings is great — some people have essentially no lipoprotein-a and some have quite a large amount, 100 mg/dl. It is said that there is a thousandfold range in the amount of lipoprotein-a. People who have very little lipoprotein-a are apt to have trouble with heart disease. The reason for this is the following:

The first step in developing atherosclerosis, which is the first step in the development of coronary heart disease, strokes, or other forms of cardiovascular disease, is a rupture of the walls of the blood vessel. The walls of blood vessels rupture in people in ordinary poor health because one of the functions of vitamin C is to strengthen blood vessel walls by the synthesis and laying down of a protein called collagen. Collagen strengthens all of the tissues in the human body. Bones would be brittle if it weren't for collagen. The bone consists of the mineral calcium hydroxyphosphate, which is brittle, and the protein collagen, which is strong and flexible. If you burn a bone in a fire, destroying the collagen, then only the calcium hydroxyphosphate is left and the bone breaks easily.

It's the collagen that makes bones and teeth tough, and makes the body tissues tough and strong. The collagen that's laid down in the walls of the blood vessel makes the blood vessel strong, resistant to lesions, and resistant to rupture. When a person dies of scurvy — not having got any vitamin C for three or four months, as happened in the old days under various circumstances — half of them die of internal bleeding from blood vessels that rupture. Before they die, they have lost their teeth because the gums have begun bleeding and have become infected. The other half of the people, those who don't die of internal bleeding, die because of infection because another job of vitamin C is to participate in the functioning of the immune system, the protective mechanism against infections.

Vitamin C is required to synthesize collagen by hydroxylating procollagen. For every hydroxyl group that's introduced, one vitamin C (ascorbate) ion is used up. In order that blood vessels, bones, teeth, skin, and other tissues can be strong, you have to have a high intake of vitamin C. This also explains why most animals continue to manufacture ascorbate. It's because animals differ from plants in a remarkable way. The animals' bodies are made strong by the protein collagen, and to synthesize collagen, you have to have a lot of vitamin C. Plants don't make collagen; they don't need it. Their structural macro-molecule is a carbohydrate named cellulose. The stalk of the plant is stiff because of the cellulose in it. So plants don't need very much vitamin C, compared to what animals need. And because of this extra need of animals to synthesize collagen, the vast majority of animals have retained the power to make their own ascorbate and do not rely on dietary ascorbate sources.

When Dr. Rath came to visit me at my home in California to tell me about lipoprotein-a, I hadn't been following this literature at all; it was all new to me. While we were talking, he made a statement that immediately attracted my attention. After telling me about lipoprotein-a he said, "You find a lot of lipoprotein-a in the blood of many human beings, and in monkeys, anthropoid apes, but not in other animals." I was astonished, and said, "Those are just the animals that have lost the ability to manufacture vitamin C."

I said, "I think that lipoprotein-a is the surrogate for vitamin C." What does lipoprotein-a do? Well, it's laid down on the walls of the blood vessels and helps to strengthen them. I mentioned that some people make practically no lipoprotein-a. Some of them die of cardiovascular disease; the blood vessels aren't so strong. They don't get much vitamin C of course, and they don't have lipoprotein-a to help strengthen the blood vessels and so they can have problems with the circulation, the blood vessels.

The range of 10-20 mg of apoprotein-a per deciliter is protective against cardiovascular disease. This range gives the optimum protection for people with the ordinary intake of vitamin C. Then there are people with more than 20 mg/dl who have overshot the mark. They start laying down too much lipoprotein-a in certain regions in the neighborhood of the heart and the brain. Why do they do that? The primary cause of cardiovascular disease is lesions to the wall of the blood vessel. These lesions occur because people have so little vitamin C that they don't make enough collagen to strengthen the blood vessels. The places where blood vessels are subjected to extra stress, as when the heart contracts and sends out a pulse of blood which forces the aorta and other coronary arteries to expand from the localized high pressure, are where lesions are more apt to occur. There is a similar phenomenon that occurs in the brain and results in strokes. This is why atherosclerotic deposits occur primarily in the regions where there are lesions in the walls of the blood vessels, these lesions being the result of the weakness caused by a deficiency of vitamin C.

Is there anything more we can say about cardiovascular disease? The people who have too much lipoprotein-a tend to have atherosclerosis because they've overshot the mark of trying to protect the blood vessels against deficiency in vitamin C and the consequent deficiency in collagen synthesis. The process of evolution hasn't yet led to the control of the level of lipoprotein-a that would be optimum for human beings. It's been shown that people who have high cholesterol in their blood die if the lipoprotein-a level is high; but they don't die if the lipoprotein-a level is low (between 10 and 20 mg/dl). Dr. Rath and I believe that we have a new understanding of cardiovascular disease, coronary heart disease, and stroke.

By the way, when Dr. Rath and I were discussing this point two years ago, that lipoprotein-a is a surrogate for vitamin C and an evolutionary compensation to repair the weakness of the arterial wall resulting from deficiency in vitamin C, I said "What about the guinea pig?" The guinea pig requires dietary vitamin C just like apes; what about its lipoprotein-a levels? The lipoprotein-a model would predict that it should be high, but it hadn't yet been measured. Dr. Rath measured the amount of lipoprotein-a in guinea pig blood and found that it *was* high, as predicted. We also found that if you put a guinea pig on a diet containing the amount of vitamin C that human beings get, it rapidly develops atherosclerotic plaques in the neighborhood of the heart. A guinea pig getting 50 times that amount of vitamin C doesn't develop these atherosclerotic plaques.

What else can we say about cardiovascular disease? One conclusion is, to prevent cardiovascular disease, you need to optimize the intake of vitamin C. That's one statement. We believe that the evidence shows, and many people working in this field have reached the same conclusion, that lesions in the walls of the blood vessels are the start of the atherosclerotic process, and those lesions result, of course, from a deficiency in vitamin C.

What else? Why does the lipoprotein-a stick to the walls of the blood vessels? Well, there is evidence — you can even do this in the laboratory — that certain groups of atoms, certain molecular sidechains, are responsible for holding the lipoprotein-a onto the walls of the blood vessels. These groups are, interestingly enough, lysine groups. Lysine is one of the 20 amino acids, one of the 10 *essential* amino acids. Everyone needs to get lysine in the diet in order to be in good health and in nitrogen balance. It is rich in some proteins, especially meat and fish, and in some vegetables, but not all. Vegetarians may be deficient in lysine. Healthy young men need 800 mg a day to maintain nitrogen balance.

In the laboratory, you can set up an apparatus with a column of material in it, to which lipoprotein-a sticks. If you then pour a solution of the amino acid lysine into the column, the lysine interferes with the combination and so the lipoprotein-a is pulled off. We predicted that lysine would be an effective means of preventing the lipoprotein-a from forming atherosclerotic plaques and might even be effective in causing the atherosclerotic plaques to re-dissolve.

I had the interesting experience a year ago of having a distinguished American biochemist come up to me and ask if I could help him to improve his health. He said he had been retired for disability a number of years ago because of heart attacks. He had had three bypass operations and he had used up his saphenous veins so that he couldn't have any more bypass operations. He would like to walk, but he couldn't walk very far, even if he took a nitroglycerine tablet at the beginning and then in the middle of the walk, without having such pain in the chest that he couldn't continue. He said he had been taking 6 grams of vitamin C because of my recommendation, so I said, "Why don't you take some lysine? You don't need to tell your physician because it's one of the amino acids. You get some in your food every day, but take some extra lysine. You can buy it. It's cheap." How much should he take? "Well," I said, "how about 5 grams a day? That would be about six times the essential amount of 800 mg. Try taking 5 grams a day."

After a couple of months, he wrote me and said it's almost miraculous. Within a month after he had reached 5 grams a day of lysine and 6 grams a day of his vitamin C, he could walk two miles without any medication, without any pain. Then a couple of months later he wrote me that he had felt so well that he had cut down a tree at his home and was cutting it up into firewood, and was also painting the house and working so hard that he again had chest pains — angina. So he went up to 6 grams a day of lysine, and he's continued chopping wood and painting the house taking 6 grams a day of lysine.

Well, I think you can understand why, for some time now, I have been in a state of euphoria. Here we have this cause of a tremendous amount of human suffering, disability, and death, suffering which affects both patients (sick and dying) and survivors (relatives and friends).

Here we have something quite new — essentially completely new. Two new ideas — that vitamin C deficiency is the primary cause, and lipoprotein-a is another part of the cause. What should we do now?

For two years we have been trying to get cardiologists and physicians to give vitamin C and lysine, and certain other substances that we know about, to cardiac patients. Very little success. We had managed to get two or three studies set up to determine the relationship between intake of vitamin C and the lipoprotein-a level in individual patients with cardiovascular disease, but we haven't succeeded in getting a vigorous effort underway. For 20 years we have been trying to get a large-scale study made about nutrients in relation to cancer. Very little success, even after 20 years.

With millions of people dying every year and millions more being handicapped by attacks of heart disease, to wait 20 years seems to us to be quite wrong, ethically. This ought to be followed up immediately.

We're not in a position to do it at our institute. Our place is too small and we don't have access to patients. We can carry out some studies, but there should be a great effort made. We decided that we would issue a call for an international effort to control heart disease. If we can cut down the mortality to 10 percent of what it is now, this would mean that people in general would live 16 years longer before they had their heart attacks. For many of them, the heart attack might be put off indefinitely. This would come close to abolishing heart disease as a principal cause of suffering and death. This international effort, involving scientists and physicians all over the world carrying out different studies, might, in a rather few years, determine just how valuable these ideas are.

This problem needs to be attacked in an effective way. Money is needed and so I agreed to help set up the Linus Pauling Heart Foundation which would be devoted to collecting money and distributing it to investigators. Its purpose would be to find out to what extent it will be possible to achieve control of cardiovascular disease now that this new information is available. I should mention that there are a hundred or so investigators all over the world who for years have been studying apoprotein-a and lipoprotein-a ever since they were discovered in 1964 by the Norwegian investigator Kåre Berg.

There has been a lot of interest in this particular lipoprotein, but until Dr. Rath and his associates did their work, this minor constituent of blood was not recognized as the culprit that's responsible for atherosclerosis. Since atherosclerosis is the start of essentially all cardiovascular disease and stroke, it is responsible for these conditions.

I hope you can understand why I am so excited at the present time about the possibilities that there can be, rather quickly, an effort that will lead to a really significant decrease in the amount of suffering in the world caused by heart disease.

Editor's note: *Dr. Linus Pauling has twice received the Nobel Prize, first for his pioneering work with chemical bonds, and second for his work with the nuclear issue. Since that time, he has devoted his attentions to the field of nutrition science and its applications to human health and disease. He works at the Linus Pauling Institute of Science and Medicine, 440 Page Mill Road, Palo Alto, CA 94306, phone 415-327-4064. Contributions to the institute are tax deductible and welcome.*

The Megavitamin Revolution

Abram Hoffer, MD, PhD

Dr. Abram Hoffer is a psychiatrist and the Editor-in-Chief of the Journal of Orthomolecular Medicine. *He pioneered, with Dr. Humphrey Osmond, the use of large doses of nutrients in the treatment of schizophrenia. In the previous article, he also introduces Dr. Linus Pauling before the Schizophrenia Foundation. This article was originally published as an editorial in the* Journal of Orthomolecular Medicine.

The test to determine whether a treatment has become popular within the medical profession is to measure the relative strength of the positive and negative assertions made about the treatment. The use of antibiotics is so well entrenched in medicine that side effects and toxicities are recognized but are accepted as the price one must pay for their positive therapeutic properties. There are no physicians who have made it their life's work merely to attack antibiotics as a crusade. In sharp contrast, vitamins which are safe even in large doses have not been acceptable to the profession, and their negative side effects have been consistently exaggerated and over-emphasized, to the point that many of these so-called toxicities have been invented, without there being any scientific evidence that these side effects are real. This pervasive negative attitude has spilled over to the news media, who have consistently followed the official line and have ignored all the claims made about the benefits of vitamins used in optimum amounts. But over the past year or so there has been a significant change in media attitude reflecting a significant change in medical opinion.

March 12, 1992, Natalie Angier wrote an article entitled "Vitamins Revitalized as Health Agents" (*International Herald Tribune*) which appeared in the *New York Times* and in the *Globe and Mail* March 14th. What is interesting in this report is not what it said, but the fact that it was said. The use of vitamins in megadoses was described without the usual massive attention to toxicity and a major warning to the readers to avoid these things as much as possible since they could get all they needed from food alone. Scientists have lost their fear of these high dosages. For example, Dr. S. N. Meydani of the Human Nutrition Research Center on Aging, at Tufts University in Boston, said, "Now we are starting to think about what is the optimal level of vitamins for lifelong diseases and to prevent age-associated diseases." This university has been headed by a nutrition scientist who at every opportunity had derided the use of vitamins in his popular columns of advice to the American public. I assume that Dr. Meydani will not be fired. The impressive results achieved by the use of vitamins is gradually overcoming the reluctance of physicians to use them, even though they might be reluctant to advise patients to take them. Thus, Dr. I. Jialal of the University of Texas Southwestern Medical Center in Dallas, is

> "...not yet willing to advise that the public start taking vitamin tablets, and he, like so many researchers, emphasizes the need for more studies. But he did admit that, given his preliminary results and the relative harmlessness of vitamin E, he himself planned to start a supplement of the nutrient daily."

I have some good news for Dr. Jialal. Up to 60% of the population are already taking vitamin supplements and have been doing so for years.

Contributors to this journal have been describing the use of optimum amounts of nutrients, including vitamins, ever since this journal was first published. Readers are not surprised by the information in the public media, and they may well wonder why it has taken so long. Angier opened her story with the following statement: "Long consigned to the fringes of medicine and accorded scarcely more credibility than crystal-rubbing or homeopathy, the study of how vitamins affect the body and help prevent chronic diseases is now winning broad attention and respect among mainstream medical researchers." She added, "They are gathering provocative evidence that vitamins influence nearly every organ, and that these enigmatic chemicals may help forestall or even reverse many diseases of aging, including cancer, heart disease, osteoporosis, a flagging immune system, neurodegeneration and other chronic disorders."

Equally interesting is the prominent attention given to these vitamins in the *New York Times*. This prestigious national newspaper has, since at least 1966, consistently ignored or criticized the use of megavitamins. This was the policy of their editorial board. Many years ago at a meeting of the Huxley Institute of Biosocial Research in New York, I was approached by a writer who had been commissioned by the *New York Times* to attend our meeting and prepare a report. He did attend for the day and one-half. This was the meeting which was greeted by Mayor Koch. At the end of the meeting this reporter approached me and asked whether I would spend some time answering his questions. I replied that I saw no point in doing so, since if he wrote anything favorable the *New York Times* would not publish. He was astounded at my statement, and reassured me that so far he had not had any of the articles, which they had asked him to write, rejected. I agreed to see him on Monday at my hotel. He came to my room mid-afternoon and stayed until 7 p.m., until my wife and I had to leave to attend the opera. He assured me that his report would appear in the Sunday Supplement within two weeks.

After several months had passed I called him to find out what had happened, and would his article ever appear. He said that the editorial board had wanted a few points clarified and could we meet again next time I was there. I agreed. Again I spent several hours with him. The story never appeared. I assumed it was favorable, although the writer did not tell me what the tenor of his report would be like. I assumed that a senior editor who had been writing major articles against the use of vitamins had killed the story. It is possible the writer was a fraud and had nothing whatever to do with the *New York Times*, but I considered this highly unlikely after getting to know him so well. This little episode merely illustrates the entrenched opposition of the *Times* to orthomolecular nutrition. They had shown similar opposition to articles written by my friend, Dr. Walter Alvarez. After a particularly critical article against psychoanalysis appeared in his column in the

New York Times, the newspaper cancelled his column. It looks as if the *New York Times* has undergone a conversion experience.

Almost every modern, acceptable treatment needed forty or more years before that treatment became acceptable. I have for many years predicted that it would take about forty years before megavitamin therapy would become widely accepted. I started the clock at 1957 when we first published our paper describing the use of large doses of vitamin B3 for the treatment of acute schizophrenia. I assumed that by the year 1997 this would become the recognized best treatment. Orthomolecular treatment originated from that particular study as one of the main roots. The other was the work by Linus Pauling who defined the term "orthomolecular" and placed his immense scientific prestige and knowledge behind the concept. His seminal work on vitamin C and the cold and flu, and more recently on the use of this vitamin in the treatment of cancer, and very recently on the role vitamin C plays in preventing hardening of the arteries, have been the most potent factor in swaying public opinion and, sometime after that, scientific opinion. But I now think that general medicine will be ahead of psychiatry, which requires much more effort to be persuaded to look at different findings and treatment philosophies.

Editor's note: *This article appeared as an editorial in the* Journal of Orthomolecular Medicine *[7(1): First Quarter 1992], the official journal of the American Association of Orthomolecular Medicine, 16 Florence Avenue, North York, Ontario M2N 1E9, Canada. Phone: 416-733-2117 FAX: 416-733-2352. Copyright © 1992 by the American Association of Orthomolecular Medicine. All rights reserved. Reprinted with permission. Author: A. Hoffer, MD, PhD, #3A-2727 Quadra Street, Victoria, BC V8T 4E5, Canada.*

The War Over
Health Freedom in America
Approaches A Turning Point

FDA Plans to Remove Amino Acids, Herbs and, Later, High-Potency Vitamins from the Market

by Durk Pearson & Sandy Shaw

Durk Pearson & Sandy Shaw are biomedical research scientists and authors of the best-selling Life Extension, A Practical Scientific Approach *(Warner Books, 1982) which sold over a million copies and inspired widespread public interest in free radicals. They have been actively engaged in research on practical methods of retarding aging since 1968. In 1990, they received the American Aging Association's Paul F. Glenn Award for "individuals who have made special contributions to biomedical aging research." The association stated, "This award serves as an expression of our appreciation of the continuing advocacy by Durk Pearson & Sandy Shaw of the promise of biomedical aging research." In addition to writing books, Pearson & Shaw also publish the* Durk Pearson & Sandy Shaw Life Extension Newsletter *which includes their informative insights into recent advancements in nutrition science, and their practical applications. Their article discusses the current political context of health freedom and the FDA's attempts to keep the American public uninformed about the scientific realities of nutrition research. [Copyright © 1992 by Durk Pearson & Sandy Shaw].*

A **fever-pitched battle** is now being waged in the halls of Congress over whether the FDA should be given draconian new enforcement powers with which to legally attack nutrient supplement and pharmaceutical companies. The FDA has revealed plans to regulate amino acids and herbs as prescription drugs, which would mean that they would be removed from the market. Gary Dykstra, head of FDA Enforcement, said the FDA will require that vitamin doses be limited to RDI levels (reference dietary intake nutrient levels, some of which are even *lower* than the current RDAs); Kessler quickly denied this, saying the FDA will permit higher vitamin doses than RDI levels unless the FDA finds alleged "safety" problems with higher doses. But you can't challenge FDA data, including safety data, in a federal court. Therefore, we can't trust Kessler and the FDA not to limit vitamin doses to RDI levels.

In Congress, the battle lines are drawn. Representative Henry Waxman's HR 3642 would vastly *expand* FDA's enforcement powers, allowing large fines on individuals or companies for not toeing the FDA line on nutrient supplement doses or health claims.

In the meantime, those who favor health freedom are battling for the passage of Senator Orrin Hatch's S 2835, which would dramatically *reduce* the FDA's powers over nutrient supplements and permit scientifically reasonable health claims. Our freedom to buy and use nutrient supplements hangs in the balance, as does our ability to extend our lifespans through the use of high-potency antioxidant nutrient supplements, which can dramatically reduce our risk of cardiovascular disease and cancer.

FDA Dead Wrong About Vitamin Supplements

Surveys have shown that about 25% of all US adults now take vitamin supplements on a *daily* basis, while 50% of all US adults use them at least sometimes. Yet, while the public's interest and enthusiasm for vitamin supplements has grown, the FDA has always taken the official position that vitamin supplements are worthless because you can get all the vitamins and minerals you need in your diet. Even now, the Public Health Service (PHS), the government agency that includes the FDA, is focusing its attention on convincing people to get nutrients from the diet, while not, at the same time, recommending that people take supplements of nutrients shown to have powerful disease-preventive effects. The PHS suggests that people eat 5 to 9 servings of fruits and vegetables a day — although only about 10% of Americans surveyed actually do this — because there are additional valuable nutrients in fruits and vegetables that you don't get in supplements.

There are, of course, other nutrients in fruits and vegetables, but that doesn't explain away any of the accumulated scientific evidence for the disease preventive effects of *individual* nutrients such as vitamins C and E, and beta-carotene, often involving amounts you can't get in even the best planned diet. The government acts as though the impressive evidence accumulated for health effects of higher-than-RDA amounts of certain nutrients (especially vitamins E and C and beta-carotene) is not as good as the far-less evidence that exists for health effects of the "other" food nutrients which they recommend so heavily. The government refuses to admit that most people should be taking nutrient supplements in addition to a good diet, probably because it would be embarrassing to admit that its anti-supplement bias has been wrong and that the health of Americans has been damaged by decades of bad advice.

A survey by the US Department of Agriculture (USDA) of over 37,000 Americans (representing a broad cross section of all Americans) reported that over 80% of Americans are not getting even the FDA's meager RDA levels of one or more essential vitamins or minerals in their diet. As data have accumulated on the health benefits of certain nutrients, especially the ability of antioxidants such as vitamins C and E and beta-carotene to reduce the risks of cancer and cardiovascular disease, the RDAs themselves are coming increasingly under attack by scientists who argue that they are adequate only to prevent classical deficiency diseases (such as scurvy) but not high enough to provide optimal disease-preventive effects.

When we wrote about how free radicals were implicated in cancer, cardiovascular disease, and even aging itself in our #1 bestseller *Life Extension, A Practical Scientific Approach* (Warner Books, 1982), few people other than scientists studying them had heard of free radicals. Now, however, the connection between free radicals and heart disease is well accepted, while a multitude of cancer researchers accept a link with many common cancers, and evidence linking free radicals with aging continues to accumulate. Free radicals are atoms or molecules with an unpaired electron, which are promiscuously chemically reactive. They are created in the body during normal metabolism, as well as by environmental factors such as pollution, cigarette smoke, and radiation. During exercise, a large increase in the internal production of free radicals takes place, which can cause injury (often resulting in symptoms such as pain and stiffness). That is why athletes and bodybuilders (or anyone else who exercises) especially need to take supplements of antioxidants such as vitamins C and E and beta-carotene.

Latest Blow to the FDA:
Vitamin C Can Increase Lifespan

A recent report of health benefits from vitamin C comes from a ten-year epidemiological study (where risk factors or lifestyle factors are correlated with mortality rates) of 11,348 Americans showing that vitamin C intakes of several hundred milligrams a day resulted in men living on the average six years longer and women living on the average one year longer. Cardiovascular disease mortality rate was substantially lower in those taking higher levels of vitamin C. You probably saw headlines in your newspaper on this study. Vitamin C is one of the body's most important antioxidants. In fact, it is concentrated in the brain and is the brain's number one protection against free-radical damage.

Studies have shown that Vitamin C can reduce platelet stickiness (when blood platelets easily clump together and risks of an abnormal blood clot that might lead to a heart attack or occlusive stroke is increased). Vitamin C also can increase HDL, the cardiovascular-*protective* fraction of blood cholesterol. Moreover, vitamin C helps prevent the free-radical autoxidation of LDL cholesterol. Oxidized LDL is now believed to be a causative factor in the formation of the foam cells that comprise part of atherosclerotic plaques.

The scientists reporting lifespan increases with vitamin C even alluded to the possibility that increased usage of vitamin C supplements by Americans may be playing a role in the sharp drop in cardiovascular disease mortality that has occurred in the US in the past 20 years or so, something with which we agree. Finally, the authors say,

> *"Based on our regression analyses, the inverse relation of*
> *total mortality to vitamin C intake [the higher the intake*
> *of C, the lower the mortality]* is stronger and more
> consistent in this population than the relation of total
> mortality to serum cholesterol and dietary fat intake,
> two variables on which strong public health guidelines
> have been issued over the years" *[emphasis added]*.

This strong comment by the paper's authors exposes the
government's bias against nutrient supplements!

Despite the evidence, the dangerous quacks at the FDA
continue to say that people do not need supplements. They
also regularly violate Constitutional First Amendment free-
speech rights by legally attacking those firms that make truthful
health claims for nutrient supplements for the "crime" of
making scientific judgments with which the FDA disagrees.
The FDA does not have to provide evidence that health claims
are incorrect in order to prosecute, and companies and individuals do not have the right, under the present system, to take
the FDA to a federal court to prove that they are wrong. The
FDA does not permit sellers of nutrient supplements or manufacturers of fortified foods (such as cereals) to make any legal
health claim for antioxidant vitamins or beta-carotene. This
policy effectively prevents firms from educating the public
about these effects. Firms who do make such claims may be
fined, have their products seized as "misbranded," or even have
company executives imprisoned by the FDA.

When Americans cannot make truthful statements, what has
happened to the First Amendment's guarantee of free speech? In
our opinion, the FDA is the single biggest barrier to the
dissemination of truthful nutritional information in America
today, as well as being a serious threat to our civil liberties and
Constitutional rights.

FDA Blocks Dissemination
of Lifesaving Information

In fact, the FDA may be responsible for over 100,000 premature deaths each year because they will not allow aspirin

companies to tell the public about the dramatic heart attack preventive effects of aspirin. Years of studies, beginning in 1948, culminated in the 22,000 physician-subject Physicians' Health Study which examined the effects of an aspirin every other day on heart attack incidence. The study was funded by the government (National Institutes of Health) and conducted by Harvard University Medical School. In 1989, the results of this study were reported in huge newspaper headlines because of the dramatic finding that the risk of a first heart attack was reduced by 44% in men over 50 who were taking an aspirin every other day. (Roughly similar results have been found in studies in which women have been included.) The sales of aspirin rose sharply. However, three months later, the sales were right back down again. Why? Because the FDA sent a regulatory letter to aspirin companies forbidding them to mention the results of this study (although widely accepted among doctors and scientists) in their aspirin advertising or labels. As a result, most people at risk of heart attack are *not* currently taking aspirin.

We have had people tell us that, since they didn't hear any more about aspirin preventing heart attacks after all the head-lines, they thought it must have turned out not to have been true. We estimate, on the basis of estimates published in the July 23, 1992 *New England Journal of Medicine* (in a survey on the effect of the Physicians' Health Study on doctors recommending aspirin and on how many heart attack patients were taking it prior to their attacks) that this ban on one truthful health claim for aspirin is resulting in at least 100,000 premature deaths from heart attacks *every year*, 20% of the 500,000 total heart attack deaths a year. Many people at risk of heart attack are not seeing a doctor regularly (many of those may not be able to afford it) and about 40% of those who die of heart attacks simply drop dead, not having noticed any symptoms before their sudden deaths. Although some people should not take aspirin — including those who are allergic to it, those who have bleeding disorders or ulcers, or those taking prescription anti-coagulants (blood "thinners") — most people over 50 should be taking a quarter to one half an aspirin daily. We both do.

FDA insiders have admitted that the agency has a bias against nutrient supplements and, despite the overwhelming evidence concerning beneficial effects of larger-than-RDA amounts of some vitamins, continues to hold to the position that nobody needs supplements and no company can make health claims for vitamins (other than that they prevent deficiency diseases) because of the loss of credibility that the FDA fears would follow if they suddenly admitted that they have been wrong for so many years. (On the other hand, they are losing credibility rapidly for continuing to hold an untenable position.) One of the members of the Food and Nutrition Board of the National Research Council (which sets the levels of the RDAs for the FDA), Max Horwitt, admitted that "Those of us who served on the Food and Nutrition Board of the National Research Council had a bias against vitamin supplements, but we are changing our view."

FDA Should Not Have Permanently Banned Sale of Tryptophan

The FDA regulates the marketing of all foods, nutrient supplements, prescription drugs, over the counter drugs, and medical devices. It has been estimated that these industries regulated by the FDA produce about 25% of the nation's GNP. It is a very powerful agency which has, unfortunately, often abused its power. A good example is the FDA's continuing vendetta against nutrient amino acid supplements. Gary Dykstra, Deputy Commissioner for Regulatory Affairs of the FDA, announced in July 1992 that his committee would recommend that the FDA make amino acids into prescription drugs. This announcement follows months of rumors and leaks.

If the FDA makes amino acids into prescription drugs (which, if it happens, would take place sometime after the 1992 election) nobody will be able to get amino acid nutrient supplements anymore, just as has happened with the essential nutrient amino acid tryptophan. They will not be available by prescription because the huge costs of receiving FDA approval (the average new drug approval cost is about $230 million) will discourage any company from investing this money in a "drug" that cannot be patented. Amino acids would simply disappear from the American market and those using them would have to switch to alternatives, including powerful prescription drugs, many of which have potentially serious side effects, and even to illicit drugs, such as anabolic steroids.

In 1989 there was a link discovered between the use of certain tryptophan supplements and the occurrence of a serious disorder, EMS (eosinophilia-myalgia syndrome), which killed about 30 people and made perhaps 1500 others very sick. The FDA rightly removed tryptophan supplements from the market when this link was discovered because nobody understood what was causing the EMS. The sudden occurrence of these EMS cases strongly suggested that it was not due to tryptophan itself, which had been on the market for decades and was being taken as a supplement by about 15 million Americans, according to the US Centers for Disease Control (CDC).

The CDC, not the FDA, is the government agency *officially responsible* for establishing the causes of epidemics. The CDC did an investigation of the tryptophan-EMS link and, in their 1990 report in *The New England Journal of Medicine*, stated that the EMS was *not* caused by tryptophan itself, but by a contaminant contained in a few batches of the tryptophan produced by one company. Years ago, when hundreds of people in Southern California died after eating soft cheese, the FDA removed all soft cheese in the Western US from the market. However, when the problem was found to be caused by contaminated soft cheese produced by one company, the FDA allowed all the other companies to put their soft cheese back on the market.

The FDA should have treated the tryptophan-EMS incident as a case of contaminated food. However, after the Centers for Disease Control published their report, the FDA did not allow tryptophan from the companies whose tryptophan was uninvolved with EMS back on the market. People who were previously using tryptophan for problems such as insomnia or bad temper have had no choice but to turn to alternatives such as alcohol and/or powerful prescription drugs, including barbiturates, meprobamate, chloral hydrate, and benzodiazepines (such as Valium®), some of which have a far higher risk of serious or lethal side effects than even the tryptophan produced by the one company responsible for the contaminated trypto-phan. *The FDA does not consider the safety of alternatives to FDA-banned substances and the resulting health costs of the use of these alternatives.*

What You Can Do to Help Stop an FDA Ban on Sale of Herbs, Amino Acids, and Other Nutrients

The FDA aims to increase its regulatory powers over all nutrient supplements, including amino acids. If the FDA bans the sale of *all* amino acids as nutrient supplements, as they have hinted for months and the FDA's Dykstra has announced, people will turn to more readily available alternatives, such as replacing supplements of the nutrient amino acid arginine with anabolic steroids, which are easy to obtain (despite the severe legal controls on them as part of the War on Drugs) and which are well known to have serious health risks.

Although there is no public health or safety issue that would justify the FDA's removal of amino acids from health food stores or mail order catalogs, that doesn't mean that they won't do it anyway. Power corrupts and absolute power corrupts absolutely. The FDA is an agency that is out of control with power lust. But even the FDA is vulnerable to political pressures. Just look at how AIDS activists have been able to pressure the FDA to approve potential AIDS drugs far faster than the FDA would otherwise have done, and to allow them to import drugs not approved by the FDA. (Millions of unor-ganized Alzheimer's patients do not have the same freedoms.)

The FDA's Deputy Commissioner for Regulatory Affairs, Gary Dykstra, was quoted in the August 9, 1992 issue of *The New York Times National* saying that the FDA has the power, under the authority of already-passed Nutritional Labeling and Education Act (the 1990 NLEA has become <u>2400</u> pages of FDA-inspired small-print regulations!), to limit the doses of vitamin supplements to no more than the RDI (reference dietary intakes, some even lower than the current RDAs) and that the FDA would not permit higher doses to be made available even by prescription. In an article the following day, *The New York Times* quoted David Kessler, Commissioner of the FDA, as saying that Dykstra was wrong and that the FDA would not be regulating vitamins in the way described by Dykstra, but that the FDA would permit sales of vitamins (although FDA would continue to permit *no* health claims) at higher-than-RDI doses as long as there was no "safety" problem at those higher doses.

Unfortunately, the FDA has the final say on what is or isn't a "safety" issue and *no one can challenge their opinion in court.* Thus, if Dykstra's interpretation of the labeling regulations is right (and as head executioner, he ought to know), the FDA could, if it chose, limit vitamin dosages to RDI levels on the basis of "safety." It sounds to us as though Dykstra let the cat out of the bag and Kessler doesn't want Americans to know about the FDA's plans because of the tremendous public outcry that would occur if the public knew.

If the new labeling regulations give them the power to limit vitamin doses to RDI levels, it is reasonable to assume that they will do so. Kessler is smart enough not to try to take over nutrient supplements all at one time. Start with amino acids, then selected herbs, and eventually move against high-potency vitamins. The FDA will avoid major opposition from the pharmaceutical industry by allowing continued sale (but disallowing most truthful health claims) of existing RDA-level vitamin products and fortified foods.

The FDA Can Be Stopped, and You Can Help

In the 1970s, when Congress received large amounts of mail opposing the FDA's plan to make high-potency (doses higher than 1-1/2 times the RDA) vitamin supplements into prescription drugs, Congress passed the Proxmire Amendments which exempted nutrient supplements from being regulated as drugs, provided that no health claims were made. Now is the time to write the White House and your Congressmen that you want to retain freedom of choice to buy and use nutrient supplements, that you do not want the FDA to regulate amino acids as drugs or food additives, that you do not want the FDA to increase its regulation of vitamins and other nutrients, and *demand* that the current Commissioner, David Kessler — who has sought ever greater FDA powers over our health freedom — be booted out now without delay and be replaced by someone more knowledgeable about nutrition, more compassionate, and more individual-freedom oriented.

How many hundreds of thousands more people will die prematurely before the FDA is finally stopped from trampling our American constitutional civil rights to freedom of speech and freedom of the press? It is especially important that you make your views known now, while Congress is considering critical legislation affecting our health freedom. You also ought to know that, according to the July 28, 1992 *FDA Insider*, Al Gore and David Kessler are buddies, and that Kessler is maneuvering to remain in office no matter who wins the election. This makes it crucial that you make your disapproval of Kessler known to both Bush and Clinton, as well as to the Congress.

David Kessler, as well as many others in the FDA, are opposed to Americans making their own health decisions. To them, the FDA does not just offer advice for you and your doctor to consider; the FDA claims to represent your best interests — whether independent scientists agree with the FDA's "science" or not, and whether you want their "help" or not — at the point of a gun. You aren't even allowed to challenge their data in a Federal court where you are represented by counsel, can call witnesses in your defense, engage in the legal discovery process to discover the scientific basis (or lack thereof) for the FDA's statements, and can cross-examine the FDA's witnesses.

As Kessler said in his article in the June 18, 1992 *New England Journal of Medicine*, "*If members of our society were empowered to make their own decisions about the entire range of products for which the FDA has responsibility...then the whole rationale for the agency would cease to exist.*" He is absolutely right! To Kessler and his ilk, the continued existence of the coercive apparatus at the FDA is more important than our rights as Americans to choose our own representatives and our

Constitutional freedoms to receive and act on data from information sources of our choice, such as peer-reviewed scientific journals, not just the FDA's self-proclaimed monopoly on truth. Kessler has said that he wants the FDA to become "the sole authority for information on health and nutrition." This medieval authoritarian attitude is extremely hazardous to both your health and to your health-care budget.

To Kessler and his ilk, the continued existence of authoritarian FDA health and nutrition czars is more important than our rights as Americans to choose our health practitioners and information sources, and act on the best information available, such as peer-reviewed scientific journals, rather than the FDA's self-proclaimed version of the truth.

Support Senator Orrin Hatch's Health Freedom Act of 1992, S 2835, HR 5561

Now is the time to let your Congressmen and Congresswomen know that you support Sen. Orrin Hatch's "Health Freedom Act of 1992" S 2835 (Senate version) and HR 5561 (House version), which would take away the FDA's power to arbitrarily regulate any nutrient food substance (including amino acids) as unapproved new drugs or as unapproved food additives, thereby protecting our freedom to buy and use nutrient supplements. Hatch's bill would also permit truthful, scientifically supported health claims, and permit those accused by the FDA of making false claims to defend themselves in Federal court. Make your support for this important bill known and demand that the bill be passed *without amendments that water down its provisions*. At the same time, register your opposition to the Dingell/Waxman/Kennedy Bill (HR 3642 and S 2135) that would vastly *expand* the police-state style enforcement powers of the FDA. The FDA is rapidly becoming an American Gestapo and they must be stopped.

Don't kid yourself. We are now engaged in a war with those who wish to take away our remaining freedom to make health decisions for ourselves, such as the right to decide for ourselves what nutrient supplements to use. A huge battle is now in progress in Congress over which side will prevail, those who want to "beef up" the FDA's powers, or those who wish to take lethally unscientific arbitrary power away from the FDA. The time to act is NOW if you want to affect the outcome.

If there are any civil-rights attorneys reading this article who have suggestions for a successful constitutional challenge to the FDA's regulation of truthful speech, please contact us in care of this book's publishers. Such a challenge may now be fruitful since the US Supreme Court unanimously upheld the First Amendment protection of commercial speech when they declared New York's "Son of Sam Law" to be unconstitutional in February 1992.

References and Notes

Vitamin C increases lifespan:
Enstrom, Kanim, Klein, "Vitamin C Intake and Mortality among a Sample of the United States Population," *Epidemiology* 3: 194-202, 1992.

Bias against nutrient supplements:
Max Horwitt quote (page 392S) in: Pryor, "The Antioxidant Nutrients and Disease Prevention — What Do We Know and What Do We Need to Find Out?" *American Journal of Clinical Nutrition*, Supplement to Volume 53, No. 1, January 1991.

Scientific consensus emerges on disease-preventive effects of antioxidant vitamins and beta-carotene at higher-than-RDA doses:
"Antioxidant Vitamins and Beta Carotene in Disease Prevention," Proceedings of a conference held in London, UK, October 2-4, 1989, *American Journal of Clinical Nutrition*, Supplement to Volume 53, No. 1, January 1991.

Dramatic reduction in heart-attack risk in men over 50 using low-dose aspirin:
"Final Report on the Aspirin Component of the Ongoing Physicians' Health Study," *New England Journal of Medicine* 321(3): 131-135, 20 July 1989.

Centers for Disease Control (CDC) reports that contaminant, not tryptophan, caused EMS:
Belongia, *et al.*, "An Investigation of the Cause of the Eosinophilia-Myalgia Syndrome Associated With Tryptophan Use," *New England Journal of Medicine* 323(6): 357-365, 9 August 1990.

FDA insiders admit FDA biased against nutrient supplements:
"L-Tryptophan: Case Study in Regulatory Abuse?" *Food & Drug Insider Report*, pages 5-6, 13 April 1992.

Eighty percent (80%) of Americans' diets deficient in one or more essential vitamins or minerals:

Pao, Mickle, "Problem Nutrients in the United States," *Food Technology*, pages 58-79, September 1981.

FDA ban on disclosure by aspirin companies of aspirin/heart attack data endangers health of Americans:

Individuals who had heart attacks but who had been "... without a history of cardiac events or a cardiac risk factor that had been identified by a physician...had a low prevalence of aspirin use that did not change significantly between January 1987 and January 1990 [one year before and one year after the publication of the preliminary and final reports on the effect of aspirin in dramatically reducing the risk of heart attacks]." Those who had a heart attack, who had been at high risk of heart attack and under the care of a doctor, had increased their use of aspirin during this period from 18.3% to 28.1%, showing that some doctors had noticed the papers and acted accordingly. Note, however, that there were still 71.9% of high-risk patients who were not using aspirin. Americans need more information about aspirin, not less. The FDA should be held *legally responsible* for deaths in which lifesaving information about aspirin that would have reached those who died and affected their subsequent behavior was withheld from the public by the FDA.

Lamas, Pfeffer, *et al.*, "Do the Results of Randomized Clinical Trials of Cardiovascular Drugs Influence Medical Practice?" *New England Journal of Medicine* 327(4): 241-247, 23 July 1992.

David Kessler claims the FDA represents you, with or without your consent:

Kessler, "The Basis of the FDA's Decision on Breast Implants," *New England Journal of Medicine* 326(25): 1713-15, 18 June 1992.

Editor's Notes: *In addition to* Life Extension, A Practical Scientific Approach, *Durk & Sandy have authored* The Life Extension Companion *(Warner Books 1984) and the* Life Extension Weight Loss Program *(Doubleday 1986). Pearson & Shaw are members of many scientific and professional associations, including: the American Association for the Advancement of Science, the Gerontological Society, the American Aging Association, the American Chemical Society, the American Oil Chemists' Society, and the Oxygen Society.*

For free information on the Durk Pearson & Sandy Shaw Life Extension Newsletter, *send your name and address to: DP&SS Newsletter, P. O. Box 728, Neptune, NJ 07754-0728. Their newsletter includes their informative and practical views on current aging research, health enhancement, their personal life-extension regimen, nutrient supplements, fat loss without caloric restriction, and improving physical and mental performance. We recommend it highly.*

Copyright © 1992 by Durk Pearson & Sandy Shaw.

In the Name of
Consumer Protection

Henry Waxman (D-CA) "protects" consumers and patients out of services and products they need. His legislation may be endangering some consumers' lives.

by Michael Onstott

Michael Onstott has been involved in the alternative health-care movement for 22 years. He became an activist in 1973 when he took part in a successful campaign to pass the Proxmire Amendments, a law which protects consumers' access to dietary supplements. A tireless advocate for freedom of choice in health care, he is currently working for people with HIV to secure the right to access natural and experimental therapies and medical devices. Mr. Onstott is the legislative chairman and lobbyist for the Natural Health Care Alliance. He is a writer and health care activist with ACT-UP San Francisco, where he is affectionately known as "Michael Vitamin."

Imagine a day in 1994 when all free-form amino acids have been banned. Many herbs like goldenseal, ephedra, sassafras, lobelia, and echinacea are only available through underground sources. Nutrients and specialized food supplements like PABA, inositol, bioflavonoids, rutin, evening primrose oil, and borage oil are unavailable in formulas or multi-vitamin products. Selenium, chromium, CoQ_{10}, and germanium are marketed in illegal clubs and back alleys. Many health food stores that sold mostly supplements have gone out of business. FDA agents, trained by undercover experts from the FBI, are shutting down holistic medical clinics, raiding warehouses filled with imported herbs, and arresting nutritionists across the country for practicing medicine without a license.

Dietary-supplement prohibition has come to America. "speakeasy"-type underground clubs and brain-nutrient parties are flourishing — a sign of deep cultural interest in the banned substances. Activists scramble to find safe sources for CoQ_{10},

N-acetylcysteine (NAC), chromium, evening primrose oil, and smuggled Chinese herbs for people with HIV, cancer, diabetes, PMS, and a host of other illnesses. Unfortunately, some people are getting sick and some are dying from contam- inated black-market amino acids and nutrients. Many products are counterfeit, containing less than the correct potency or containing none at all. Other people are dying because they cannot find sources for the nutrients and herbal therapies that had been benefiting them.

This prohibition-era scenario may seem farfetched, but the legal and regulatory machinery to bring it about is already in place. Additional laws are pending that will make this picture not only possible, but likely. Dietary supplement prohibition is possible because the Food and Drug Administration (FDA), along with apparently well-intentioned consumer protection-ists, are leading an attack on alternative health care in an effort to punish the "quacks" and "snake-oil salesmen," and prevent health consumers from making "wrong" choices. This sincere effort to "clean up" the health food industry is beginning to circumvent the rights of consumers to choose their own health care.

The Nutritional Labeling and Education Act

In 1990, Congress passed the Nutritional Labeling and Education Act (NLEA), a law which Henry Waxman co-sponsored, to encourage informed consumer choices in regard to nutritional supplementation, diet, and positive life-style changes. Congress liked the way in which high-fiber-decreases-colon-cancer and low-saturated-fats-decreases-heart-disease claims had modified consumer choices. NLEA was supposed to encourage (and regulate) the process. Unfortunately, the US Food and Drug Administration was charged with the respon-sibility of writing the NLEA regulations, and they thwarted Congress' intentions. Instead of protecting consumers and assuring that they have access to safe products and truthful information, the FDA is demanding a stringent standard of proof for all dietary-supplement health claims comparable to their standard for approving new drugs.

This drug-approval standard, if enforced, would force almost all dietary supplements off the market because of the costs of testing products as "new drugs" are so high — 20 to 250 million dollars — that only major corporations can afford the process. Product development would be effectively restricted to the medical establishment. Not only would vitamins and herbs with limited markets be shut out, but the legal difficulties of obtaining a patent on the "generic" vitamins and herbs would guarantee that no company would undertake the financial investment in the first place. Most dietary supplements would go away, never to return.

FDA Leadership in Action

The FDA's Commissioner, Dr. David Kessler, has provided the moral leadership that has led the FDA (in conjunction with state and local authorities) to raid a holistic medical clinic in Kent, Washington, seventeen health food stores in Texas, a Utah-based herb company distributing evening primrose oil, Nutricology of San Leandro, California, a dietary supplement company in Oregon, a black-currant oil distributor in Illinois, the Life Extension Foundation in Florida, herbalists in northern and southern California, and many other small- and medium-sized businesses throughout the country. Despite the FDA's inexperience in the field of evaluating dietary supplements, they have the power to control that which they do not understand — and they are using it.

The "new" Kessler FDA has a friend in Los Angeles-based Congressman Henry Waxman, who is also a man with a mission. Waxman has introduced legislation that, when combined with other House bills and the FDA's NLEA regulations, could set American society up for an era of dietary prohibition akin to the speakeasy days of the "roaring twenties."

Consumer Protection vs Access to Health Care

Consumer protection is a complex issue, given the social and political realities of America in the '90s. The current battle pits the strict protectionists against those who call for greater access and the right to choose one's own health care. It is a struggle between those who prefer government intervention and regulations to assure safety and efficacy and those who advocate *informed self-responsibility* and expanded access to drugs and natural therapies which can benefit their health. Poor recipients of Medicaid, people with HIV, AIDS, cancer, Alzheimer's and other life-threatening diseases — as well as consumers of dietary supplements, herbal products and alternative therapies — are often dismayed to learn that some of the people working to protect their rights to access various types of health care may be sabotaging those very efforts. This tragic circumstance is no better personified than in the ambitious and almost visionary work of Congressman Henry Waxman of the 24th Congressional District in Los Angeles. Savvy in the ways of political power, Waxman is a master legislator, unrelenting in his push for apparently laudable goals. His legislative ambitions may take years to achieve, but he does not give up until the obstacles before him are finally swept aside.

As an example of his tenacity, after nearly ten years of delays, Waxman helped push Congress to pass comprehensive clean-air legislation — a significant achievement, given the final compromise with some of the more conservative forces representing Detroit's auto industry. Waxman also helped pass bills to expand Medicaid coverage for poor women and children, provide money for AIDS treatments, and to mandate nutritional labeling (the NLEA). He has recently withdrawn his FDA-enforcement bill (HR 3642) which would have significantly empowered the FDA to seize and embargo "fraudulent" or "harmful" products without warrants or court orders. Waxman, a formidable foe to the anti-regulatory Republicans, fights daily to pass government regulations that "attempt" to guarantee safety and efficacy. Unfortunately, much of his legislation seems to backfire.

Quality Health Care?

Henry Waxman, a self-proclaimed protector of the poor, objects to requiring Medicaid recipients to use "managed care." Although 45% of workers with employee-paid health insurance participate in managed health care plans, Waxman insists that any lower-income citizen (Medicaid recipient) should be free to access the services of any doctor she or he chooses. In reality, however, the poor have very few choices when it comes to Medicaid practitioners. Medicaid's considerably decreased rates strongly discourage physicians from accepting Medicaid patients. Representative Ed Towns (D-NY), a member of Waxman's Health and Environment Subcommittee, says, "freedom of choice becomes meaningless when there are few or no willing providers." In Town's Brooklyn district, for instance, only 18 out of 331 qualified doctors will treat Medicaid patients.

Janet Novack, in an article on how Waxman and his Congressional allies unwittingly helped to drive up medical costs for virtually everyone on government assistance programs, points out that "many on Medicaid go to low-quality Medicaid mills or hospital emergency rooms, or put things off, which can mean that they later need more expensive care." In his continuing resistance to managed care, Waxman has led Congress to limit the health-care choices of poor women, children, and the elderly. If Waxman's vision of genuine access to any doctor of choice could be realized, patients would truly benefit. Individuals could choose physicians who practice allopathic or holistic medicine. Unfortunately, Waxman-sponsored legislation unwittingly restricts rather than expands choices for individuals seeking health care.

More Orphan Drugs?

Henry Waxman has sponsored amendments to the Orphan Drug Act. Orphan drugs are unpatented drugs that treat rare or otherwise untreatable life-threatening diseases. Waxman's amendments, intended to control excessive corporate profits, in fact, "curb the development of new AIDS treatments" according to activist Jim Driscoll in an article for the *Wall Street Journal.* Waxman's "anti-research and anti-business" amendments limit patient access to new and promising treatments because drug companies will not develop drugs they believe to have extremely limited marketability. Dr. Driscoll points out that "two of Mr. Waxman's amendments do especially grave harm. One retroactively cancels the market exclusivity of an orphan drug when epidemic conditions raise the theoretical patient population above 200,000." The other bill disallows orphan drug status if forecasts put the theoretical patient population above 200,000 within three years. Since Congress can and does politicize science by changing the rules for drug development in the middle of the game, access to potentially beneficial drugs and to AIDS research itself is put in jeopardy by Waxman's amendments.

Upping the Ante

More recently, Henry Waxman, Representative John Dingell (D-MI), Senator Edward Kennedy (D-MA), and Senator Orrin Hatch (R-UT), have sponsored the Prescription User Fee Bill, which would require drug companies to ante-up $150,000 to develop any new drug. Smaller and newly emerging entrepreneurial companies developing cutting-edge, state-of-the-art drugs and therapies are seriously and selectively disadvantaged by this arbitrary expense. To the big drug companies, $150,000 only slows them down a bit. By upping the drug-development ante, companies will tend to develop only those drugs which are "sure things" in terms of marketability. Many promising and potentially life-saving drugs will likely fall through the cracks of this ill-conceived consumer-protectionist scheme.

In seeking to punish or penalize "big business," Waxman legislation frequently discourages major corporations from developing products that could benefit consumers. Waxman deals in the arena of the powerful corporations, the "medical establishment." His legislation rarely succeeds in promoting product development by smaller-sized companies, and often the reverse. Waxman's power is funded by contributions from the Medical Establishment and he tends to exclude smaller and alternative health care companies from his considerations.

More FDA Power

Henry Waxman's HR 3642 (the Food, Drug, Cosmetic and Device Enforcement Act), drafted by Waxman's counsel, Bill

Schultz, empowers the FDA to embargo or seize herbs, dietary supplements, or amino acids without a warrant for up to 30 days. HR 3642 further empowers the FDA to fine herbalists, practitioners, manufacturers and store owners for selling nutrients not approved by the FDA, such as specific medicinal herbs, evening primrose oil, certain B-vitamins, chromium, CoQ_{10}, etc. Fines up to $250,000 for individuals or $1,000,000 for manufacturers could be levied. The seizure-and-embargo or penalty powers are enough to drive a smaller company completely out of business. The constitutional guarantee of *due process* becomes meaningless for some companies; even if they win their case, they lose. Companies are unable to sue an agency of the government for recovery of court costs, which can run anywhere from $30,000 (bare minimum) to many hundreds

of thousands of dollars (more typical). Although HR 3642 does not specifically refer to dietary supplements, FDA empowerment can be used against providers of herbs and natural health products.

Reinforcing Ignorance

Since FDA officials are most often recruited from the medical/pharmaceutical and law-enforcement fields, general ignorance about nutritional supplements is widespread. With this prejudice, it is not hard to understand why harassment against those who sell or prescribe supplements is on the rise. Herbal and nutritional therapies — which are often based on preventive and quality-of-life concepts like balance, purification, detoxification, prevention, and healing — have been characterized by FDA officials as "fraudulent" and "a waste." At a Congressional hearing in Washington, DC, called "Recent Trends in Dubious and Quack Devices," chaired by Congressman Ron Wyden (D-OR) and Ed Roybal (D-CA), all of the witnesses were hostile to the natural health-care industry. One witness, Dr. Renner, indicated that the following percentages of "quacks" are present in the following professions:

Dieticians	. 0.2%	Chiropractors	60%
M.D.s	1%	Health Food Stores	80%
Nurses	1%	Herbalists (& naturopaths)	. 80%
Dentists	1%	Acupuncturists	90%
Pharmacists	. 1%	Homeopaths	98%

Another friend of the FDA and admirer of Commissioner David Kessler is Dr. Victor Herbert. Herbert is a member of the board of the National Council Against Health Fraud (NCAHF) and co-author with Steven Barrett of *Vitamins and Health Foods: The Great American Hustle*. Dr. Herbert calls acupuncture "quackupuncture" and refers to homeopathy as "a scam based on nonsense principles."

Empowering Ignorance

Given the FDA's philosophy in regard to herbal and dietary supplements, HR 3642 would empower an already-biased FDA to harass businesses and practitioners who provide herbs and nutrients (including amino acids) to people with HIV and cancer, and to harass consumers whose choice is alternative health care. The so-called "vitamin raids" on Dr. Jonathan Wright's holistic medical clinic in Kent, Washington and seventeen health food stores in Texas are ample evidence that the FDA's 40-year war on alternative health care options is alive and well in the "new" FDA.

Politics as Usual

Waxman has steadily increased his political influence by helping liberal colleagues win elections. His "political machine," co-founded with friend and fellow politician Representative Howard Berman, taps the huge financial resources of the Los Angeles liberal community. In 1989-90 alone, his office estimates that he "shared" $220,000 with fellow Democrats, many of whom are members of his subcommittee on Health and the Environment, of the House Committee on Energy and Commerce.

Waxman receives a large portion of his "war chest" PAC money from the industries his legislative committee is charged with regulating. When the vote on HR 3642 came up in full committee, all 27 Democrats voted in favor, and all 16 Republicans voted in opposition. Of a recent total of $829,000 total PAC money, Waxman received over $356,000 from the medical, pharmaceutical and insurance industries. By contrast, fellow Democrat and Chairman of the full House Committee on Energy and Commerce, John Dingell (D-MI), received only $18,000 from PACs associated with medical and pharmaceutical industries. Waxman's opponent for election in California's newly formed 29th district, Mark Robbins, received only $9,800 in total contributions, none of it from PAC sources. Enough Democrats from Waxman's district have become so upset with Waxman's brand of politics that they have formed the Democrats-for-Robbins Committee.

In the Dark?

Is Waxman's congressional staff "protecting" him from the facts? Waxman has claimed that he was unaware of information brought to his attention in correspondence he says he did not receive. Further, his Los Angeles and Washington, DC, staff have recently been known to answer inquiries incorrectly about the status of his own legislation. Occasionally, when legislation is about to be acted upon, staff members have said that the legislation was "in limbo."

Despite his protestations, it seems unlikely that Waxman's professed ignorance of FDA intentions and activities relating to implementing the NLEA implementation is really a staffing problem. When tens of thousands of consumers from around the country responded to his proposed legislation HR 3646 with anger and frustration, he should have investigated the political-social-cultural realities surrounding that response. Consumers feel threatened by FDA empowerment bills because *they don't trust the FDA*. They also don't trust Congress or any other federal bureaucrats to determine what sort of health care they should or shouldn't choose, or what specific nutrients and herbs they should or shouldn't use.

Waxman knows that the FDA can use the proposed "modernizing" and "necessary" powers granted by HR 3642 to harass legitimate providers of alternative health care products and services out of business. But he has consistently claimed ignorance on the issue of the FDA's biased agenda in regard to dietary supplements. He would have us believe that he does not understand how the FDA would use its new powers through the NLEA and HR 3642 to empower the medical establishment over alternatives, increasing its control over access to health care in this country.

What Consumer Protectionists Think of Consumers

Henry Waxman, financed by the medical and pharmaceutical industries, appears to distrust the very consumers he says he is protecting. He has said that the issue of access to alternative health care, specifically regarding the safety and efficacy of dietary supplements, is too complex for consumers to understand. He believes that those who use alternative health products are the collective "children" and Congress and the

FDA are the collective "parents." Since consumers are too naive and inexperienced to make intelligent choices, then "mommy" (the FDA) and "daddy" (Congress) must help guide the "children" to assure that they make "beneficial" choices and do not hurt themselves in the process.

With this view, Waxman has infantilized the issue of consumerism. Bureaucratic paternalism is almost inevitability destructive in a society in that it disenfranchises citizens. The

"children" must be brought to the table and their experience, knowledge, and concerns respected.

Since Congress is the FDA's boss, legislators have a responsibility to be informed about health issues, consumer needs and concerns. If the law-makers don't understand the science in this case, they at least need to understand the consumers who benefit or suffer as a result of their enacted laws. Lawmakers also have the absolute obligation to get more than one opinion on scientific matters, especially in regard to alternative health care or newly emerging research. The FDA, if they *really* want to protect the health and welfare of US citizens, has the moral duty to expand and diversify its sources of knowledge and opinions, especially in the field of dietary and herbal supplements and newly developing health devices.

The Drugs-and-Guns Mentality

Since half of those who work for the FDA are recruited from the medical/pharmaceutical industry and half come from law enforcement, the agency has a "drug and guns" mentality which guides its policy and enforcement activities.

Henry Waxman's brand of corruption does not seem insidious to many insiders because they idolize the "good works" he does and agree with his well-intentioned philosophy. They say "it's a liberal political machine working for the good of the people." But the fact remains: Waxman is being paid off by the health-care industry that he helps regulate. In his quest to protect the consumer for whom he has little respect, he defers to the "scientists" at the FDA for regulatory decisions. These FDA-approved scientists, weaned on orthodox medical biases favoring symptomatic relief via drugs and surgery in the treatment of disease, consistently reject alternative ideas as quackery. FDA scientists expressing tolerance are discouraged, demoted, or fired — if they are ever hired in the first place. The FDA has little respect for traditional or nutritional therapies or the consumers who use them. We are faced with a tremendous dilemma here; those charged with protecting our health care rights and needs do not understand or respect us or the health care we seek. This must change.

Identifying the Hidden Intentions

Tenacious, forceful, and patient, Henry Waxman has the best of intentions. Unrelentingly myopic, he has consistently stated that HR 3642 is not intended to restrict access to dietary supplements. He seems to be saying, in essence, that Kessler and the FDA, even though they could, will not use the power that HR 3642 provides against any legitimate business. Although Waxman's imagination may be inadequate to the task, others have no problem imagining what the FDA will do with the power it has been dreaming about for decades. Enough honest legitimate Americans have *experienced* the FDA's true intentions, without the temptations of Waxman's enforcement bill.

Who is Really Misinformed?

Recently, Waxman "tabled" HR 3642 from consideration after witnessing an overwhelming negative response from consumers and the health food industry alike. Nonetheless, Waxman's philosophy of consumer protection has found strong proponents among many Democrats in Congress. Waxman and some of his fellow lawmakers characterized the initial response as a "misinformation campaign" orchestrated by the health food industry. Proponents of HR 3642 thought that consumers were misled by health food stores to believe that Waxman's legislation would directly restrict access to herbs and supplements. Ultimately, consumers' concerns regarding potential ramifications from the FDA empowerment bill were justified, even though HR 3642 does not specifically refer to dietary supplements.

The FDA's stepped-up agenda of selective harassment may seem appropriate to those who favor strong government intervention, but not to most consumers. Waxman has consistently characterized his legislation as not restricting "vitamins in any way." In a recent letter to clarify issues and allay fears of restricted access, he said, "To make this absolutely clear, I have amended the bill to state that it will not in any way affect the authority of the FDA with respect to vitamins and supplements." Actually, Bill Richardson (D-NM), not Henry Waxman, amended HR 3642 with language that reaffirms the Proxmire Amendments and the NLEA, which was intended to guarantee access to supplements.

The issue of protecting access becomes very complex, however, because the FDA intends to declare many products to be "unapproved drugs" due to health claims, or "unapproved food additives" with unproven safety. Henry Waxman occasionally seems incapable of seeing the potential ramifications of his legislation. HR 3642 may say nothing about supplements, but it certainly could be used to limit access to many medicinal herbs, amino acids, and "new" supplements such as evening primrose oil and CoQ_{10} which have been used safely for years (some herbal products for centuries). Since Waxman is not likely to give up the idea of increasing FDA enforcement powers, HR 3642 will probably be re-introduced in slightly amended form for consideration by the new 103rd Congress.

Consumer Endangerment?

Dr. Kessler also publicly states that "we [the FDA] are not trying to shut down health food stores." Unfortunately, given the current thrust of FDA activities, HR 3642 will more than likely provide the FDA with even more temptation to use its power to limit access to supplements. Since motivated consumers and people with life-threatening illnesses will not relinquish access to herbs and supplements, black markets will surely flourish to supply the public's need for embargoed or banned products. In other words, over-regulation is the same as total de-regulation. In a black-market economy, consumers would have no assurance of safety or purity, but many would be quite willing to take a chance in order to acquire supplements that had worked for them in the past. Consumer endangerment is certainly no intention of Henry Waxman or the FDA. However, intentions are only intentions; the reality of the FDA's interpretation and implementation of HR 3642 is quite another matter. Henry Waxman and those who would "protect" consumers should consult first with the consumers themselves. Waxman's view that consumers are not experts in the field of dietary supplements is ironic. In fact, many users of supplements are far more expert than the average FDA official. Henry Waxman's unfortunate mistrust of the consumer and his misplaced trust in so-called experts has led to an antiquated brand of consumer protectionism that not only fails to protect consumers but blocks access to valuable services and products and prevents the development of new treatments and drugs that could be improving the quality and duration of many consumer's lives.

A New Democratic Vision

Critics of Henry Waxman's legislation come from the political left, right and center. Potential allies have been lost because Waxman's philosophy promotes the idea that government is morally and intellectually capable of "protecting" consumers. Waxman believes in government as the people's advocate. He thinks that the activities of business should be restricted and channeled to benefit consumers and recipients of health care. Unfortunately, the web of moneyed influence, political power, and bureaucratic incompetence, ignorance and bias, combine to sabotage well-intended efforts to truly serve and respond to the needs of the public.

With Bill Clinton's relatively upbeat campaign for the presidency, many Americans were looking to the Democrats for a "new vision." Clinton alluded to this socio-political leap of faith and commitment to working together when he spoke of a new American "covenant." Even some Republicans seem to understand the crucial need to explore the political parameters beyond legislative and bureaucratic paternalism and welfarism that entrap and can ultimately destroy its so-called "beneficiaries." We need to move toward genuine citizen participation and enlightened self-responsibility, to an era of informed consumerism. In regard to the health crisis which threatens to bankrupt our country by the turn of the century, we must begin to involve people in their own health process. Biotechnology, nutritional and medical research, computerization, and increased access to information will make investment in education and new technologies imperative. Our society cannot financially or socially afford to pay insensitive bureaucrats to take health consumers by the hand [or throat] and lead them every step of the way through their personal health process. In our "information society," new knowledge must flow and government agencies must not be provided with the right or the ability to censor or distort that which is known. The old liberalism of Henry Waxman, Ted Kennedy, and Ralph Nader will hopefully give way to the new vision of Senator Tom Harkin (D-IA), Congressional candidate Mark Robbins (R-CA), and others who believe that health consumers not only have the right to choose, but that practitioners and scientists must work directly with consumers, and all must be respected as experts in their own right.

Editor's Note: *The prescription User Fee Bill passed the House and Senate in October with a provision that exempts smaller pharmaceutical corporations from the $150,000 drug-development fee.*

Michael Onstott is active in the Natural Health Care Alliance of San Francisco, a non-profit health advocacy organization dedicated to the promotion of responsible natural health care. You can reach them at NHCA, 1348 La Playa Avenue #2, San Francisco, CA 94122, Phone: 415-731-8115, FAX: 415-731-3850.

Waxmangate:
Why Americans Hate Congress

Paul A. Gigot, *The Wall Street Journal*

It's only fitting that Caspar Weinberger was indicted in the same week that Ross Perot leads in the polls and Washington celebrates the twentieth anniversary of Watergate. All three events are related, as Henry Waxman understands.

The diminutive Mr. Waxman is the Little Big Man of Congress' "Watergate class" of 1974. Though virtually unknown outside Washington, the Los Angeles liberal is one of the most important American politicians of the past 20 years.

The reforms, so called, that Watergate ushered into Congress help explain Mr. Waxman's brilliant career. His career helps explain the "gridlock" in Washington that has voters turning in desperation to Ross Perot.

The 92 freshmen in the Class of '74 first overturned discipline inside the Congress, with Henry Waxman in the vanguard. They deposed old barons and created multiple sub-committees to disperse power. In 1978, just four years on the job, Mr. Waxman became the first member to defeat a more senior colleague for a subcommittee chairmanship.

In 1974, only a month before he resigned, a besieged Richard Nixon signed a landmark budget "reform." It diminished a president's power to influence spending choices, while handing new power to such legislative entrepreneurs as Mr. Waxman. Budgets could be assembled in one giant "reconciliation," typically at the last minute. A single shrewd operator with enough votes could suddenly make even a president blink.

"Henry Waxman walks around this place with proxies from 150 Democrats in his pocket," explains California Rep. William Dannemeyer, the ranking (and admiring) Republican on Mr. Waxman's subcommittee. Congress' leaders may want to compromise, but Mr. Waxman can prevail by focusing those proxies on key priorities. A budget director who wants a broader deal at any cost (Dick Darman) is putty in his hands.

Little Big Henry has thus been able single-handedly, and all but invisibly, to turn Medicaid from a welfare supplement into an entitlement cascading toward $100 billion a year. And because Medicaid is partly funded by state governments, Mr. Waxman can personally take credit for forcing many state tax increases. Even Bill Clinton, of all people, has accused Mr. Waxman of imposing national health care via Medicaid and using "the states' credit cards as the financing mechanism."

Mr. Waxman's greatest genius, though, has come in political finance. The Watergate "reforms" were supposed to purge private "fat cats" from politics. Instead they created congressional fat cats who learned how to exploit the political-action committees (PACs) of special interests.

Mr. Waxman is fatter than most. Though he has a safe seat himself (even this year), he has still raised millions from PACs. (In 1991 alone, according to Common Cause, Mr. Waxman received more PAC money, $348,950, than all but one other House member. Most of it is protection money paid by the businesses he regulates from his subcommittee.) Why? The answer goes back to those Democratic proxy votes. Mr. Waxman raises money to ladle it out to other Democrats running in competitive seats. In 1989-90 alone, his office figures he bestowed $220,000 on liberal colleagues. Those members don't forget who buttered their permanent incumbency. It's no wonder Mr. Waxman now rivals Chairman John Dingell in choosing who can sit on his Energy and Commerce Committee. Mr. Waxman is assumed to be Mr. Dingell's heir apparent as well.

Watergate's aftermath was supposed to humble an arrogant executive, and it did, though at the cost of strengthening an arrogant and unruly Congress. Its staff has grown with its ego, to 31,000 now from 20,000 in 1972.

The nastiest expression of its arrogance is the use of "independent counsel" to terrorize executive branch officials, even those like Caspar Weinberger who've long ago left office. That law too was passed in the wake of Watergate. Does anyone think a Henry Waxman would let such a law pass if it also applied to him?

All of this might be just another story about how Washington works, except that voters are concluding it doesn't work. While Mr. Waxman can pass his personal agenda, his very success precludes Congress as a whole from passing a sensible budget. And while voters have elected Republican presidents, ingenious liberals managed to exploit the Watergate reforms and burrow into a tenured Congress that seems unaccountable.

Disgust with Congress suggests the public agrees with Gerald Ford. "All they did was screw it up," the former president and House GOP leader recently said about the post-Watergate reformers. The House now, he added, is composed of "435 prima donnas who have no allegiance to their party or their leaders."

Mr. Waxman will still be in Congress in 1993, but perhaps so will enough new members to reform the House that Watergate Built. Term limits and redistricting have already upset the stranglehold of Mr. Waxman's political operation in his home of California. If we're lucky, 1992 will be the beginning of the end of the Waxmangate era.

Editor's note: *Mr. Gigot's "Potomac Watch" column originally appeared in the* Wall Street Journal, *Friday, June 19, 1992. Copyright © 1992 by* The Wall Street Journal, *reprinted with permission. All rights reserved.*

The Power of Information

by Will Block

Will Block is a biomedical researcher with extensive expertise in electronic database searches.

It's an old saw that freedom requires responsibility. Unfortunately, many of our political leaders are quick to jump in and translate responsibility as regulation. Where would we be, if freedom were — gulp! — unrestricted? But the conclusion that freedom requires some slavery is absurdly reducible and quite as nefarious as: "In order to save the town, we had to destroy it!"

If we're going to save ourselves from the stranglehold of this specious reasoning, we're going to need some "response-ability." Consider the value of the study by Enstrom,[1] and published recently in *Epidemiology*, showing that a relatively small amount of vitamin C can add six years to the life of men and one year to the life of women. Consider the hundreds of positive, peer-reviewed, double-blind, placebo-controlled studies on the benefits of beta-carotene in cardiovascular disease, or anti-oxidants in cancer, or folic acid in neural-tube defects. There is no substitute for the power of scientific papers to clarify the advances of preventive nutritional science and to demonstrate the stark contrast with the often-overwhelming hazards of many drugs. Yet there are those with great power who would stem that advance by limiting the flow of valid and important scientific information.

It has been estimated that the amount of accumulated knowledge in the biomedical sciences is doubling every 5 years and, in some specialties, as rapidly as every 2 years. Certain fields are transforming so rapidly that many biomedical professionals, who have not kept pace with the flow of new information, are finding the limitations of their knowledge to be beds of quicksand.

Enter Electronic Databases

Electronic databases are enormous compilations of many thousands of worldwide scientific publications, some stretching back 20 years or more, and stored in large-scale computers. Consisting of abstract summaries, key words, indices, author/ publication information, and even full text, biomedical databases are updated frequently and, in some instances, even prior to official publication dates. United by a common indexing scheme, accessing these databases via local computer networks from inexpensive and powerful personal computers is now both practical and economical for those not funded by government grants or by large research organizations.

This means it is possible for an independent scientist or an intelligent lay person to amass the currency of research which hitherto required the drudgery of a medieval monk. This tool makes it far easier for the inquiring mind to get an overview of the complex maze of scientific knowledge. Thus armed, it becomes rapidly obvious which lines of scientific inquiry are dead-ending or doomed to extinction, and which are blooming and hopeful. This knowledge permits scientific research to be more accurately aimed and to better build upon its successes. Although we are only just entering the adolescence of electronic scientific database researching, the future is bright with the probabilities of even more rapid and sustained health advances.

Only one thing can help reduce the calamity of a society plummeting into health-cost bankruptcy: properly promoted preventive programs. Yet restrictions on the flow of information about nutritional health advances only serves to enhance the upwardly spiraling cost of health care and dims prospects for the infirm and aging. Widespread information about the Enstrom study on vitamin C and heart disease could save hundreds of thousands of lives, and billions of dollars in health care and disability costs. And there have been literally thousands of other scientific papers reporting information that could substantially reduce many of the infirmities of aging and usher in a new era of health — but only if people can hear about them and make up their own minds.

By its very nature, human knowledge is constantly evolving; even the best science is subject to amendment and greater contextualization. But to concede a monopoly on truth to a government agency acting as absolute scientific czar is fraught with peril far exceeding that of so-called snake-oil information governments so fear. This is true even when government is close to the actual target, as has certainly been the case with its emphasis on fat reduction. Even here the FDA doesn't know how to handle new information, such as that showing that stearic acid, a saturated fat found in substantial amounts in

meats, decreases serum LDL cholesterol. In addition, the FDA's labeling rules do not permit a separate listing for monounsaturated fats, which have different properties from either saturated or polyunsaturated fats. Monounsaturated fats, such as are found in large amounts in olive oil, are believed to contribute importantly to the reduced incidence of cardiovascular disease found in those eating a Mediterranean diet. The FDA continues to support labeling that promotes increasing the consumption of polyunsaturated fats to reduce serum cholesterol, even though human epidemiological and intervention studies show no decrease in cardiovascular disease. Furthermore, many studies in experimental rodents have shown that the higher the level of polyunsaturates in the diet, the higher the incidence of tumors developed by the animals. The FDA is many years behind the times on the science of dietary fat.

Simply by permitting food- and nutrient-supplement companies to inform the public of reliable scientific evidence for the disease-preventive effects of antioxidants (most notably, vitamins C and E and beta-carotene), 100,000 premature deaths could be prevented in the U.S. every year.

In the meantime, information is available to those who seek it out. Scientists can still publish their unorthodox data, and computerized databases make them readily available to anyone. In the end, it is those who, on their own, ignore the medical bureaucracy's claim of a monopoly on truth and seek out the most comprehensive and up-to-date scientific information who will win the day with prolonged and healthier lives.

Reference

1. Enstrom JE, Kanim LE, Klein MA. Vitamin C intake and mortality among a sample of the United States population. *Epidemiology* 3: 194-202, 1992.

Editor's note: *Will Block performs database searches for a modest fee. He is a source for over 2,000 existing searches at significantly reduced prices, many of which are continually "topped off" with the latest information. For a brochure outlining the service, discussion, and/or price quotes, call him at 908-922-8611 (FAX: 908- 922-6818).*

The AIDS Drug Underground, AIDS Activists, and the FDA — A Historical Overview

by Paul A. Sergios

This article is based on Paul Sergios' autobiographical history of the AIDS underground, One Boy At War: My Life in the AIDS Underground, *soon to be published by Alfred Knopf (scheduled for April 1993). Mr. Sergios lives in Ft. Lauderdale, Florida and is a regular contributor to* Forefront – Health Investigations.

The most significant political influence on FDA policy in recent history was brought to bear by AIDS activists and the leaders of the AIDS treatment underground. These two groups, working separately and in tandem, have forced the FDA to selectively back down from its enforcement activities. They compelled the FDA to create the Personal Importation Policy which allowed AIDS and other patients to import FDA-unapproved drugs for their personal use, they pressured the FDA into openly tolerating a nation-wide network of AIDS buyer's clubs (selling unapproved drugs, foreign versions of US prescription drugs, vitamins and nutrients for the treat- ment of AIDS), and they have proposed legislation which would expedite the approval process of still-experimental drugs for life-threatening diseases.

The Early Years

The origins of the AIDS underground and their political influence dates back to the early years of AIDS. Shortly after the discovery of HTLV-III (HIV) as the probable cause of AIDS, there was a sense of elation on the part of many PWAs (people with AIDS or ARC [AIDS-related condition]). The discovery of a virus which selectively infected CD4 lymphocytes (immune cells) seemed to be a straightforward cause for the suppression of cell-mediated immunity characteristic of AIDS. PWAs were optimistic that anti-retroviral drugs would be rapidly screened and that effective therapies, perhaps even a cure, would be just around the corner.

This early optimism was short-lived. Disappointment and mistrust began to surface in 1985 and 1986 as it became clear that only one drug, AZT, had emerged as a potentially effective anti-HIV agent. And when AZT's effectiveness was found to be marginal — and its toxicity severe enough to prohibit many HIV-infected persons from using it — PWAs began to express frustration. Where were all the immuno-modulatory and anti-viral drugs that were promised by the medical mainstream? Why were so many of the emerging clinical trials focusing on nucleoside drugs like AZT, such as ddI and ddC? Why did they have such narrow inclusion criteria — criteria that prohibited most AIDS patients from participating?

This attitude of frustration and suspicion of the slow-moving medical mainstream on the part of AIDS patients was further compounded by widespread apathy and helplessness on the part of private-practice AIDS physicians. Most physicians' knowledge of AIDS treatments was limited to standard AZT-based approaches. Most were unaware of alternative approaches that did exist, and most were unwilling to even monitor patients who wanted to use unapproved drugs and unproven therapies. Out of this psychological and social climate, the AIDS underground drug movement emerged.

The Emergence of the Underground

As early as 1984, people in the HIV and gay communities began taking matters into their own hands. Several underground chemists, working independently, began scouring the European medical literature for possible approaches to thwart HIV and to rebuild the cell-mediated (T-cell) immunity lost in the virus' wake. These individuals, including Steve Gavin of Baltimore, Rob Springer of Santa Monica, David Mitchell of Pacific Palisades, and Jack Gerhardt of Seattle, found the means to synthesize moderately large quantities of such compounds as DTC (Imuthiol), AL-721, and DNCB, none of which had been approved for human use by the FDA. The chemists distributed the drugs to patients in the community while tracking their progress.

Other individuals, such as Jim Corti in Los Angeles and David Wilson in Jacksonville, found international sources for other potentially promising agents, many of which had shown *in vitro* (test-tube) activity against HIV. They imported and sold large quantities of the compounds which included Dextran Sulfate, N-acetylcysteine and ddC.

Many patients traveled to Mexico to obtain quantities of Ribavirin and Isoprinosine, both of which had shown preliminary efficacy in treating AIDS. A San Francisco-based patient advocacy group, Project Inform, imported large quantities of the drugs. Following a protocol suggested by the underground researcher Sam Murdoch, Project Inform designed an optimum dosage schedule for the drugs and published and distributed fact sheets detailing this information. Many individuals self-medicated with the drugs following the Project Inform guidelines. Project Inform tracked many of the patients' responses to the medication and issued a report to the community in 1987 that showed that two-thirds of the people who took the medications experienced a slowing in the deterioration of their condition — though no cure.

Rejection of the Status Quo in the Mainstream Research Community

In early 1989, Project Inform launched a controversial underground study of a drug called trichosanthin, an extract of the Chinese cucumber root, which would come to be known as Compound Q. In a sophisticated screening assay, the drug seemed to have the ability to destroy HIV-infected cells (lymphocytes and macrophages) while leaving uninfected cells unharmed. The drug was being evaluated in official government-sanctioned studies at one location, but only a few patients would be administered the drug, and only at infinitesimal and possibly sub-therapeutic dosages.

The resulting community outrage at the lack of a large-scale study (that should have been designed to rapidly gather information about the drug's optimum dosage and its best method of administration), as well as community pressure to provide early access to the medication for AIDS and ARC patients, prompted community leaders to decide that the only expedient and ethical course of action was to conduct an underground research study.

Physicians in four cities participated in the trial. No standing Investigational New Drug (IND) permit was filed with the FDA. No Institutional Review Board (IRB) passed judgment on the protocol. (An IRB is a committee of physicians, lay people, clergy, and attorneys that approves and periodically reviews experimental protocols to ensure that the rights of human subjects are protected. Although no standing IRB reviewed the Q protocol, the study was adjudicated by a committee of medical and legal professionals assembled by the principal investigators themselves.) The study was designed in an open collaboration between patients, physicians, research scientists, and community activists.

The results of the study showed that trichosanthin may have some value in stabilizing the conditions of certain ARC and HIV-asymptomatic patients, but that it also poses a risk for patients with HIV-related neurological dysfunction. The study's clandestine nature, as well as its methodology (which lacked a placebo control group), drew fire from the mainstream medical establishment. One south-Florida researcher commented, "This is fear and suspicion of the medical establishment out of control."

Despite the renegade study's seemingly anti-establishment nature, leaders of the unorthodox research project met with FDA officials and presented a summary of the trial's results. It was one of the first occurrences in which the AIDS treatment underground shared research findings with regulatory officials.

Shortly after the completion of the underground trial, a number of underground Q clinics sprang up across the country, with individual physicians and volunteer nurses administering the medication, monitoring for possible toxicity, and tracking patients' progress.

The Rise of the American
AIDS Buyer's Clubs

By late 1989, the AIDS drug underground had become increasingly organized and sophisticated. "Buyer's clubs" sprang up in almost every major American city. These ostensibly not-for-profit institutions sold experimental and promising anti-HIV medications to PWAs under the terms of the 1988 Personal Importation Policy which allowed local FDA discretion for individuals wishing to import a three-month supply of a medication from anywhere in the world — provided that the drug was for his or her personal use and that it would be taken under the supervision of a physician. The buyer's clubs found sources in international markets for such non-approved drugs as Fluconazole and oral Alpha-Interferon. They purchased the drugs in quantity, then redistributed them at costs substantially lower than standard prescription drugs. The buyer's clubs also imported drugs already approved in the United States but whose prescription price made them economically prohibitive for many PWAs. The anti-retroviral drug ddC, for example, which retails for $150 a bottle, is still available from the New York buyer's club, the PWA Health Group, for a cost of $45 a bottle.

In some cases, buyer's clubs distributed extensive lines of herbal and nutrient supplements that had shown efficacy against HIV, against viral disease in general, or against the multitude of nutrient deficiencies associated with HIV infection. These supplements included vitamin C, N-acetylcysteine, glycyrrhizin (licorice extract), B-complex vitamins, CoQ_{10}, egg lipids, antioxidant formulas, bioflavonoids, and multi-vitamin and multi-mineral supplements.

Although the FDA has been completely aware of the existence of the buyer's clubs and their activities — even to the extent of interceding with Customs relating to importations of overseas drug shipments — the buyer's clubs were not and are still not regulated by the FDA or any other agency. Although the FDA has recently announced plans to conduct investigations into the activities of the buyer's clubs, it has yet to announce any change in its multi-year "hands off" policy regarding the activities of the AIDS underground.

The Political Activists

The activities of the AIDS treatment underground coincide with the rise of various activist organizations such as ACT-UP (the AIDS Coalition To Unleash Power). Founded by playwright and author Larry Kramer, the group's original mission was to use every weapon at its disposal to fight for the release of promising experimental drugs for AIDS. Civil disobedience, protests, and meetings with high-level FDA and NIH officials to effect permanent policy changes were all part of ACT-UP's agenda.

Challenging the Drug Companies

Days after the Burroughs-Wellcome Company announced that AZT's price tag would be close to $10,000 per year for one patient, ACT-UP members donned blue pin-striped suits and bogus nametags and crashed the New York Stock Exchange. One minute before business was about to begin, they chained themselves to the railing overlooking the trading floor and unfurled a banner that read *Sell Wellcome*. They then made obstreperous noises — disrupting trading for hours. They were eventually removed by police, but thousands more continued to march in protest outside the stock market doors. Weeks later, Burroughs-Wellcome reduced the price of AZT to about $6,200 per year.

In 1989, at the final meeting of the Lasagna Committee hearing, ACT-UP members James Eigo, Dr. Iris Long, and Mark Harrington delivered a stunning critique that summarized the FDA's inadequacies, and, in particular, how its supervision of AIDS drug development and clinical trials of anti-HIV medications were grossly inappropriate. Harrington then read 12 demands from what would become a historical manifesto. Among those demands were the right to use prophylaxis for opportunistic infections in government-run clinical trials, the banning of the use of placebos, the use of points other than death as outcome variables in clinical trials, and the incorporation of the patient as an active participant in the design of clinical trials.

Representatives of ACT-UP were successful in convincing the FDA to speed approval of ddI and to approve the anti-CMV drug ganciclovir without a placebo-controlled trial.

Congressional Influence

In 1991, ACT-UP Golden Gate's James Driscoll co-authored a bill entitled the "Access to Life-Saving Therapies Act," submitted to Congress by Representative Tom Campbell (R-CA). The legislation would have allowed pharmaceutical companies to market experimental drugs after completion of phase-1 trials which had shown promise of efficacy and manageable toxicity. Under the provisions of the bill, the drugs could be withdrawn from the market by the FDA should they later prove unsafe or ineffective in phase-2 or phase-3 studies. By lowering drug-development and drug-approval costs, the bill would have provided strong economic incentives for fledgling companies to compete with their larger counterparts in developing drugs for life-threatening diseases.

If you'd like to receive information on Mr. Sergios' articles in Forefront, *write to: MegaHealth, P. O. Box 60637, Palo Alto, CA 94306. Phone: 415-949-0919.*

The Nutritional Labeling and Education Act (NLEA)

by James L. Beck

James L. Beck is the founder and President of Solaray, a large supplement-manufacturing company located in Ogden, Utah. He is also on the board of Utah Natural Products Alliance (UNPA), a manufacturer's lobbyist group [see chapter by Claire Farr].

The reason the FDA and others who make up the medical monopoly want to see the supplement industry regulated out of existence is because it is becoming so successful that it is a genuine threat to the "economic turf" that the mainstream medical profession and large pharmaceutical companies have come to believe belongs exclusively to them. Their monolithic empire has no room for alternative ideas about health, nutrition, and prevention when it threatens their pocketbook.

The FDA's NLEA Regulations

On November 27, 1991, proposed regulations were published in the Federal Register pursuant to the Nutrition, Labeling and Education Act (NLEA) which had been passed into law the prior year. In reading these voluminous proposed regulations, it became clear to me that the FDA had cleverly corrupted the intent of Congress with language designed to change the rules under which dietary supplements would be regulated. These new rules, if ultimately adopted, would make it virtually impossible for a supplement to qualify as a candidate for a health- or disease-related claim. The FDA proposed that:

> "the substance must retain its food attributes at the levels that are necessary to justify the claim. For example, if the substance is a vitamin that must be present at a therapeutic level for a health benefit to occur, the supplement would not qualify for a health claim under this proposal. A therapeutic level of a vitamin would be far above that

level that is normally characteristic of food, and, consequently, the vitamin would not retain its food attributes." [1]

The FDA is not defining that upper limit.

This is a neat and well-disguised "Catch 22" that the FDA has proposed in order to drastically restrict possibilities for health claims for vitamin, mineral, or herbal supplements. In many cases, a dietary supplement provides a benefit *precisely because* it supplies a particular nutrient in a potency much higher than that which would be found in food.

Furthermore, the agency states that "food components that are modified to such an extent that they no longer retain their food attributes will also not be eligible to be the subject of a health claim. If claims are made for such components, the agency may well regard the components as drugs." [2] Of course, the FDA could (and most certainly would) use this to prevent claims for a host of products now found in health food stores.

As if these were not enough barriers to prevent the dietary supplement industry from making beneficial health claims, the FDA goes on to say that the substance for which the claim is made would have to "...contribute taste, aroma, or nutritive value..." [3] where "nutritive value" is defined by the FDA as "value in sustaining human existence by such processes as promoting growth, replacing loss of essential nutrients, or providing energy." [4]

These prohibitions are clearly absurd on their face. For example, people generally take supplements *because* they are concentrated and convenient, and in many cases because they want to *avoid* flavor and aroma. Most consumers of odor-controlled garlic capsules consume them specifically for those reasons. Also, the narrow definition of "nutritive value" is designed to unnecessarily limit and restrict entry.

For food products generally, the FDA also proposes to prevent claims for any of the combination products that have become so popular in health food stores. The FDA says:

"A food labeled under the provisions of this section shall be deemed to be misbranded under section 201(n) and 403(a) of the act if its labeling represents, suggests, or

implies ... that the food has dietary properties when such properties are of no significant value or need in human nutrition. Ingredients or products such as rutin, other bioflavonoids, para-aminobenzoic acid, inositol, and similar substances which have in the past been represented as having nutritional properties but which have not been shown to be essential in human nutrition may not be combined with vitamins and/or minerals, added to food labeled in accordance with this section, or otherwise used or represented in any way which states or implies nutritional benefit." [5]

Just in case a product — by some miracle — gets past these road blocks, the FDA has established the ultimate barrier. It has proposed that any claim for a dietary supplement have "significant scientific agreement" [6] among qualified experts and that the FDA must approve any such claim *in advance*. This is the agency's way of severely restricting claims for dietary supplements. Their position will be that there cannot be significant scientific agreement about the validity of a claim *if the FDA does not agree*. The FDA will virtually never agree. They almost never have in the past because of their bias against the industry, and the proposed NLEA regulations are proof of the agency's undaunted bias to this day. The FDA's approval of osteoporosis prevention claims for calcium should not temper our concern because the evidence was so overwhelming that the FDA would have become a laughingstock within the scientific community had they not done so. The FDA has only decided to allow this dietary supplement claim for calcium after the claim is of no value. Very few companies even care to mention the osteoporosis connection on their calcium products because it is now common knowledge — common knowledge derived from media coverage of the issue, despite FDA resistance. Freedom of speech in the *press* is still protected in this country.

The proposed NLEA regulations were the final straw in the haystack of harassment this industry has endured. In 1976, the Proxmire legislation had to be passed into law in order to prevent the FDA from regulating vitamins and minerals as drugs. Unfortunately, this law does not protect herbs and other substances like evening primrose oil and CoQ_{10}. The Proxmire legislation did not prevent the FDA from exploiting loop-holes in the law that have allowed them to seize and remove products from the market by simply calling them "unapproved food additives," even when there was no evidence that the product was unsafe.

Perhaps one reason the FDA attacks the supplement industry is because the FDA grows in size and power when large pharmaceutical companies spend hundreds of millions of dollars to substantiate safety and efficacy for new synthetic, patented drugs — all of which must be approved by the FDA. For natural products, however, you rarely find companies willing to spend even a fraction of this amount to gain new drug approval for a substance that is unpatentable. Without a patent, they don't get market exclusivity and cannot recoup their investment.

These may seem like serious accusations, but why else would the FDA act in such a biased fashion towards the nutrition industry? The FDA and the mainstream medical profession have supported and participated in a systematic attempt to destroy the credibility of the supplement industry. They have colluded with the American Dietetic Association's tireless crusade to co-opt (and dominate exclusively for themselves) the right to provide nutritional information to consumers. They have opposed the development of alternative health-care professions. On August 25, 1987, Federal Judge Susan Getzendanner, in U.S. District Court, found the American Medical Association had engaged in an illegal boycott against chiropractors and an injunction against such activity was entered and affirmed by the U.S. Court of Appeals for the 7th Circuit on February 7, 1990.

The practice of Naturopathy is very successful in such states as Washington and Oregon. However, simply because these health-care physicians believe in treating people with nutritional supplements and other natural methods, the AMA lobbied against them and has been successful in preventing their profession from achieving legal status in all but a few states.

The mainstream "FDA-medical" *monopoly* exists and thrives with less and less competition thanks to laws passed by well-meaning legislators who are not well informed about the many safe and effective natural methods of preserving health and combating disease. This is being done despite the fact that more and more people are seeking alternative health-care practitioners and products, as noted in *Time* magazine's November 4, 1991, cover story on "Alternative Medicine." A consumer poll taken by *Time* indicated that 84 percent of patients *would go back to an alternative doctor* for additional help.

The August 1989 Federal Trade Commission (FTC) report, *Health Claims in Advertising and Labeling,*[7] clearly shows that allowing reasonable claims in a competitive market enhances the consumer's awareness and behavior in a beneficial way. For example, this report states:

> *"Overall, the evidence from this study on advertising's ability to add information to the market is important for the current debate on the desirability of allowing health claims in food advertising. While this study does not provide any definite conclusions about the most appropriate policy towards producer advertising of health claims, the study does document that the potential benefits of permitting this type of advertising may be substantial. Restrictions on manufacturers' ability to communicate the health effects of fiber cereals appear to have limited the public's knowledge of the fiber/cancer issue and restricted the information's spread to certain groups within the population. Our evidence suggests that had producer advertising never occurred, fewer individuals would be eating cereal and other fiber products, and those eating cereal would be eating lower-fiber cereals. This effect would be most pronounced for non-whites, smokers and women who live in female-headed households.*
>
> *One concern about health claims in advertising is based on the presumption that, because manufacturers will only high-light favorable aspects of their products,*

consumers' purchase decisions will be made worse by advertising that is not required to disclose unfavorable nutrition characteristics. However, the evidence from the cereal market suggests that in some cases competitive forces may correct for this type of individual producer bias. For instance, all producers whose cereals contained all but the lowest levels of fiber were induced to label fiber content voluntarily. Moreover, despite the focus on the health benefits of fiber, cereals became "healthier" in other dimensions as well during the fiber/health advertising period. The average levels of sodium and fat in high-fiber cereals continued their downward trends throughout the advertising period. These and other health dimensions became the focus of advertising in the competition among high-fiber cereals."

One of the few doors of opportunity that has theoretically been slightly open for a few natural products has been in the area of over-the-counter (OTC) drugs. However, this door is rapidly closing because the FDA is in the final stages of closing the monographs for all OTC categories. They have apparently taken the position that a drug would have to go through the extremely restrictive "new drug application" process to be approved before it would be allowed. Again, from a practical standpoint this virtually eliminates any possibility for a non-patentable, natural substance.

However, even when the monographs were open, the FDA was opposed to the approval of natural substances for the treatment of disease conditions. For example, when the FDA closed the monograph on benign prostatic hypertrophy (enlarged prostate) it concluded that surgery is the only effective treatment for this condition.[8] In reaching this conclusion it disapproved a proposal that PA 109 (sabal), an extract of the herb *Serenoa repens*, be approved for treating enlarged prostate.

Both of the reviewed clinical studies were "double-blind, randomized, and placebo-controlled." The FDA concedes that the reviewed clinical studies were "well controlled" and resulted in "statistically significant improvements." However, in analyzing the results of these studies, the FDA takes the rather bizarre position that even though the improvements in symptoms were statistically significant, they were not "clinically significant." For example, the FDA states:

> *"Although the Champault study suggests that patients treated with PA 109 showed some statistical improvements in the symptoms associated with benign prostatic hypertrophy, the results are not considered clinically significant, i.e., the symptoms continue to exist and the patient is not medically better. The decrease with PA 109 in the mean number of nocturnal micturitions (nighttime urinations), from 3.12 to 1.69, compared to 3.12 to 2.7 for the placebo, may be statistically significant; however, the reduction represents a decrease of actually only 1 micturition, which the agency does not consider to be clinically significant."* [9]

I am sure that if you asked a person with an enlarged prostate, he would most definitely consider it to be "clinically significant" <u>to him</u> if he had to get up one less time during the night to urinate.

The reviewed studies also showed statistically significant improvement in increasing "mean urine volume" and reducing "residual urine." Again, the FDA states that these improvements are not "clinically significant," because they do not compare with the results achieved through surgery. The FDA would never let anyone else get away with such an "apples-to-oranges" comparison.[10]

In rationalizing their position, the FDA states that:

> *"...as long as only the symptoms of the condition are relieved, individuals who fear surgery may be lulled into a false sense of security and thus delay reexamination by a physician, resulting in a delay in treatment of the disease. Therefore, the agency believes that providing symptomatic relief without eliminating, arresting, or treating the obstructive causes of benign prostatic hypertrophy will mask the potential of the condition's progression and result in delayed diagnosis of secondary*

complications, i.e., stagnation of residual urine, urinary
tract infection, and potential renal damage." [11]

This statement demonstrates the FDA's low regard for the intelligence of consumers. It also demonstrates the FDA's unwillingness to consider education of the consumer as having any merit. A fairly simple warning statement on the label could alert consumers to the need for periodic reexamination. Surgery is not normally elected until the symptoms become quite severe. This means that millions of men who could otherwise have many years of symptomatic relief (at minimum), are being denied that choice because the FDA doesn't believe the consumer is intelligent enough to make correct choices. Sabal herbal treatment is what millions of European men choose every year. Shouldn't the US citizens have the same right to choose?

The FDA also states that "a full characterization of what comprises the liposterolic extract of sabal used in various studies would be necessary in order to describe the ingredient in a drug monograph." [12] This is simply another ploy that the FDA uses to exclude *natural* substances from genuine consideration in the drug-approval process. Natural substances can simply not be *fully* characterized in the same manner as a pure synthetic substance. Natural substances are by their very nature extremely complex. They can be standardized based on generally agreed upon markers of activity (or concentrations of specific components), and this can assure consistency, safety, and efficacy. However, as long as the FDA insists upon a *full characterization*, they have — in reality — shut the door on natural products.

When I read the FDA's proposed NLEA regulations in early December 1991, it was clear to me that corrective legislation would be required to *force* the FDA to deal with the food supplement industry more fairly. As it turned out, this was just the type of legislation that Senator Hatch wanted to introduce. Hatch was well aware of the FDA's bias and had realized that new legislation was required. When he discovered how important this issue was to dietary supplement consumers in the State of Utah, as well as the nutritional supplement industry, he decided not only to introduce corrective legislation but to support it vigorously. Senator Hatch's Health Freedom Act of 1992 hit the country like a thunderbolt. Thousands of letters and phone calls from concerned citizens from all over the country came into Congress asking them to co-sponsor Hatch's bill. These consumers were telling their legislators that they wanted the freedom to choose what type of health care they wanted for themselves, and furthermore, that they wanted access to information about the benefits dietary supplements had to offer. Even though it was nearing the close of the 1992 session for Congress, a great number of senators took the time to study this issue and co-sponsor Senator Hatch's bill. Congressmen Bill Richardson and Elton Gallegly both introduced companion bills in the House. These also quickly gained co-sponsors.

If the "Health Freedom Act" becomes law it will establish:

1. A broader definition of the term "dietary supplement," to include herbs and other substances.
2. That dietary supplements are not drugs.
3. That dietary supplements are not food additives. This will force the FDA to regulate dietary supplements on the basis of genuine safety concerns rather than the FDA's own biases. The Federal Food, Drug, and Cosmetic Act (FD&C Act) would be maintained completely intact with regard to the FDA's authority to remove any poisonous or deleterious substance from the market.
4. That truthful, non-misleading information that is based upon scientific evidence will be permitted. It seems strange that in this country we should actually have to pass a law to allow this, but that's how distorted FDA regulations have become.
5. That prior approval by the FDA of truthful and non-misleading claims is not required.
6. That a warning letter from the FDA claiming that a company is in violation of the FD&C Act can be challenged in federal court. For example, if the FDA sends a warning letter to a company alleging that it is making a health claim for a product that the FDA believes is false or misleading, that company would have the right to bring an action in a U.S.

court so that the matter can be evaluated in an independent judicial review process.

This "Health Freedom Act" finally sets forth regulatory rules that are fair and reasonable. If passed into law, it will create a renaissance of creative investment in the development of products that can substantially bring down the skyrocketing cost of health care while at the same time improving the health of millions of consumers who are anxiously awaiting the time when they can freely participate in a system in which they have access to health-promoting and disease-preventing products as well as information about those products.

This legislation will become law if the millions of citizens who care about this issue let their legislators know how they feel. Please continue to call and write your Senators and Representatives until they understand how important this issue is to the health and well-being of all Americans.

Remember, "The price of freedom is eternal vigilance."

References

1. 56 Federal Register p. 60545.
2. 56 Federal Register p. 60546.
3. 56 Federal Register p. 60563; proposed section 101.14(b)(3)(i).
4. 56 Federal Register p. 60563; proposed section 101.14(a)(3).
5. 56 Federal Register p. 60393.
6. 56 Federal Register p. 60563; proposed section 101.14(c)(2).
7. Federal Trade Commission; August, 1989; Health Claims in Advertising and Labeling - A Study of the Cereal Market pp. 117 and 118.
8. 55 Federal Register p. 6929.
9. 55 Federal Register p. 6927.
10. 55 Federal Register pp. 6927 and 6928.
11. 55 Federal Register p. 6929.
12. 55 Federal Register p. 6928.

Editor's note: *James L. Beck can be reached at: Solaray, Inc., 2815 Industrial Drive, Ogden, UT 84401. Phone: 801-621-5631. FAX: 801-621-2961.*

FDA — Friend or Foe of Our Nutrition?

Kirkpatrick W. Dilling, Attorney at Law

Kirkpatrick W. Dilling is an attorney specializing in FDA law. He is licenced to practice law in the US Supreme Court, Federal Court, and eight states. He is General Counsel to the NCIH and the Cancer Control Society, and is Director of the Adelle Davis Foundation. Mr. Dilling is active in numerous community issues and is listed in Who's Who in America, Who's Who in Finance and Industry, Who's Who in the World, Who's Who in the Midwest, Who's Who in American Law, Dictionary of International Biography, Men of Achievement, *and* Personalities of the West and Midwest. *This article was written just after introduction of the Hatch Health Freedom Act.*

Of special interest in the field of public health is the US Food and Drug Administration, the agency which is intended to serve as custodian and guardian of the public interest as it pertains to a pure and nutritious national food supply. Its activities include responsibility for administering federal food and drug laws which vitally affect the health of the nation. Regrettably, the vast powers of the FDA have been too often employed to trample upon the civil rights of regulated firms and individuals, particularly those marketing vitamins and other dietary supplements. These practices are wholly out of tune with current-day concern for individual freedoms and democratic processes. The result is actual harm to good nutrition for the American public.

In the FDA's Washington headquarters, there is a large portrait of Dr. Harvey Wiley, crusader and mentor of the 1906 Food and Drugs Act which preceded the present Food and Drug statutes. Before the turn of the century, Dr. Wiley had observed the extent to which certain interests purveying patent medicines, dangerous products, and other detrimental substances had created a national situation which cried out for remedial legislation. With his "poison squads" publicizing the situation, Dr. Wiley was able to secure passage by Congress of the Food and Drugs Act of 1906. However, to his great disappointment, Dr. Wiley witnessed, over the years, perversion of the new laws by those (such as Coca Cola and the bleached-flour interests) which the law had been intended to control. In 1929, Dr. Wiley wrote his classic *History of a Crime* detailing perversion of the food and drug laws by various monopolistic groups, and the consequent harm to American nutrition. Dr. Wiley wrote in conclusion:

> *"The resistance of our people to infectious diseases would be greatly increased by a vastly improved and more wholesome diet. Our example would be followed by the civilized world and thus bring to the whole universe the benefits which our own people had received. We would have been spared the ignominy and disgrace of great scientific men bending their efforts to defeat the purpose of one of the greatest laws ever enacted for the protection of the public welfare. Eminent officials of our government would have escaped the indignation of outraged public opinion because they permitted and encouraged these frauds on the public. The cause of a wholesome diet would not have been put back for fifty or a hundred years."*

Although the FDA currently purports to honor Dr. Wiley, in truth it continues to pervert the principles for which he stood. For many years, the FDA, under the guise of "protecting the American consumer" and "saving" him from spending his money for the "wrong" purposes, has sought to promulgate dietary regulations and/or legislation which would ban scores of dietary products that have been sold for years in an open and competitive marketplace throughout the United States. In effect, these FDA proposals would, if successful, substitute a Washington-dictated diet for the freedom of choice we now enjoy. These proposals, if implemented, would bar American citizens from freely employing such products. The FDA's "diet police" would obviously be in excess of any authority granted by Congress and in violation of various provisions of the United States Constitution as well.

The FDA's actions inevitably favor interests detrimental to optimal national nutrition. As our national food supply has increased in abundance and variety, there has been an increasing trend towards consumption of "convenience" foods which, by virtue of nutritional losses incurred through processing, refining, cooking, storage and other factors, fail to provide good nutritional value. Unquestionably, foods containing proper nutrition are *available* to everyone. However, the ordinary person has little knowledge of nutrition. Statistics reported by a select committee appointed to study the FDA show that, conservatively, more than 75 billion dollars in baked goods, cereals, flour and macaroni, soft drinks, alcoholic beverages, and confectionery is sold each year in the United States. Total consumption of these foods — which are high in "empty calories" and low in (if not devoid of) nutritious vitamins, minerals, and other essential nutrients — has been steadily rising. The consumer is greatly influenced toward these "nutritionless" food selections by steady mass-media advertising.

Nevertheless, in recent years a nutritional revolution has been sweeping over the country. Coupled with a rising general concern for the environment, there has been a growing realization that malnutrition and inadequate diet are problems affecting people from all walks of life. The eminent nutritionist Dr. George Briggs has stated:

> *"The American public is eating a strange diet. We feed our farm animals better, giving them all of the vitamins and minerals we take out of the foods for humans."*

Dr. C. Edith Weir, Assistant Director of the Human Nutrition Research Division of the US Department of Agriculture, adds:

> *"Most of all the health problems underlying the leading causes of death in the United States can be modified by improvements in diet. Public awareness of these problems has been augmented repeatedly through published national dietary surveys. One national dietary survey published by the US Department of Agriculture noted that approximately one-half of US families fail to receive the nutrition vital for their best health."*

Understandably, to help meet these problems, notable scientists have urged supplementation of the diet with vitamins, minerals and other nutritional substances. For example, Dr. Roger J. Williams, past Director of the Clayton Foundation Biochemical Institute at the University of Texas, pioneer nutritionist, and discoverer of pantothenic acid (vitamin B_5), stated:

> *"It is my viewpoint that each individual has a substantial responsibility for ordering his own life, including his consumption of food. If each will take advantage of the unity of nature, diversify his food, avoid too much refined food, cultivate body wisdom, and use nutritional supplements when informed judgment so dictates, I am sure that better health will be the reward."*

In view of these circumstances, one would expect that the US Food and Drug Administration, the agency charged by law with impartial and non-discriminatory administration of federal food and drug laws, would favor all measures for improving the nutritional pattern of the American public. However, due to pressure of vested interests and repressive policies adopted by its officials, the vast power of the US Government has too often been employed to discriminate against those making dietary products available. Meanwhile, the FDA issues deceptive statements intended to divert public attention from what is transpiring. FDA Commissioner David Kessler recently stated, for example: "It is not our business to tell people what to eat."

L-Tryptophan

L-tryptophan is an essential nutrient and constituent of proteins found in foods. Recent FDA actions denying tryptophan to consumers provide a good example of biased, illegal and discriminatory FDA procedures.

Since late 1989, the FDA has conducted an intensive campaign to bar L-tryptophan to the public, including a nationwide campaign of "trial by publicity" to convince the public that L-tryptophan is "dangerous" and should not be consumed. FDA officials responsible for this campaign have carefully chosen to ignore the facts, also failing to advise the public that there is no government legislation "banning" L-tryptophan, nor has there ever been a judicial decision against it.

These FDA officials have known all along that there has never been any safety problem with L-tryptophan, even with consumption by many millions of people for decades. L-tryptophan is an important component of the foods we eat, and is required by everyone for health, even life itself. However, to destroy L-tryptophan consumption, the FDA has falsely publicized the recent incidence of a rare blood disorder, Eosinophilia Myalgia Syndrome (EMS), as being caused by L-tryptophan instead of a contaminant. The US Centers for Disease Control have officially determined, for the record, that a contaminant was responsible, and the identity of the contaminant has been established and published. The FDA does know these facts, yet they persist in their falsehoods.

The June 1991 official FDA publication *FDA Consumer* contained a short statement (buried amongst other texts):

> *"Epidemiologic studies indicated that a vast majority of the EMS cases were linked to products containing L-tryptophan produced by Showa Denko K.K. However, it appears that the problem is not with the amino acid itself, but rather with the product becoming contaminated as a result of a change in the firm's manufacturing process"* [Emphasis added].

Concurrently, the FDA is also conducting its suppressive actions against such nutritional substances as enzymatic CoQ_{10} and sesquioxide germanium, a valuable dietary mineral.

To insure maximum "Big Brother" impact against its targets, the FDA has employed "SWAT teams" which swoop down on clinics and small businesses, intimidating workers, employees, patients and customers, and seizing their products, books and records. As illustrations of these tactics, see FDA actions against Dr. Jonathan Wright's Clinic (Kent, Washington), Century Clinic (Reno, Nevada), and Natural Vision (Manitowoo, Wisconsin).

More Authority for FDA?

Incredible as it may seem, the FDA is actually attempting,

through legislation proposed by friendly legislators such as Congressman Waxman and Senators Metzenbaum and Kennedy, to give itself even more authority.

A Legislative Remedy

However, there are Washington legislators who appreciate some of the real problems involved and who oppose granting the FDA almost-unlimited additional authority. Among these is Senator Orrin Hatch of Utah, who has introduced Senate Bill 2835, which, if enacted, would deter FDA discrimination against dietary supplements. Senator Hatch is also the principal author of an amendment to the Nutrition Labeling and Education Act of 1990, intended to exempt dietary supplements from some of the general procedures and standards applicable to other foods. Senator Hatch noted that different treatment was warranted for dietary supplements because of "the important role of vitamins and minerals in maintaining a balanced diet and in helping to prevent certain serious illnesses and health problems." He also stated:

> *"By their very nature, the dietary supplements must be marketed so that the consumer is informed of the health and disease-prevention benefits that may be conferred. Greater flexibility is thus required to permit communication of these benefits. This increased regulatory flexibility is also mandated by the very rapid pace of scientific advances here and abroad linking the prevention of long-term disease to improved nutritional supplementation."*

Enactment of Senator Hatch's "Health Freedom Act" deserves the support of every concerned American, so as to prevent further misuse of bureaucratic power which has accompanied the L-tryptophan situation and other recent matters involving our nutrition.

Editor's note: *Kirkpatrick W. Dilling lives in Illinois. Write to him at: 150 North Wacker Drive, Chicago, IL 60606. Phone: 312-236-8417. FAX: 312-236-8418.*

The Curious Continuing Ban of L-Tryptophan: The Serotonin Connection

by Dean W. Manders, PhD

Dean W. Manders holds a PhD in sociology from Brandeis University. He teaches on the adjunct faculties of several schools in the San Francisco Bay Area, including the University of San Francisco and the College of San Mateo. When not teaching courses at local colleges or writing articles, Dr. Manders practices as a nationally certified conflict mediator. This article is his latest report.

In the fall of 1989, the amino acid tryptophan was much in the news. Numerous cases of a relatively new and debilitating health disorder causing muscle and joint pain, thickening of muscles and skin, and various flu-like symptoms — Eosino-philia-Myalgia Syndrome (EMS) — had surfaced in individuals using L-tryptophan. To date, more than 1,500 cases of EMS have been recorded in the United States. Moreover, 38 deaths have been attributed to L-tryptophan implicated EMS.

In response to the outbreak of EMS, the Food and Drug Administration pulled L-tryptophan off the market on November 17, 1989, and banned the distribution and sale of L-tryptophan on 22 March 1990. Following this action, the incidence of EMS cases dropped off rapidly. Presently, the FDA status of L-tryptophan is an "Investigational Unapproved New Drug." As such, L-tryptophan is not legally available for sale to the public anywhere in the United States.

The fall 1989 media furor over L-tryptophan and EMS has passed. However, between then and now, significant investigations and events have taken place in regards to the entire issue of L-tryptophan, EMS, and the FDA. This information warrants public scrutiny and discussion. For as will be seen, in the light of such information, it seems most likely that the reputation of L-tryptophan has been needlessly destroyed.

And what has been lost is not merely the "good name" of L-tryptophan. No. In truth, public access to a powerful and safe aid to combat psychological anxiety and depression, as well as to facilitate pain control, is presently denied to the American public.

Background

L-tryptophan is an amino acid, a protein building block of life. From the late 1960s to the fall of 1989, L-tryptophan was widely sold in tablet, capsule and powder forms as a nutritional supplement by vitamin companies in health food stores and other retail establishments. From the late 1970s, L-tryptophan was also used by pioneering medical practitioners looking for non-drug answers to patients' physical and psychological problems. Such practitioners realized that once inside the body, L-tryptophan can produce serotonin, an important brain neurotransmitter.

Prior to the EMS epidemic of 1989, the safety record of L-tryptophan was outstanding — in this country alone, since the late 1960s, millions of people have used L-tryptophan safely. The effects of L-tryptophan-generated serotonin in the human body are: 1) substantial reduction in pain sensitivity; 2) effective relief of many cases of depression, without drugs; 3) soothing of anxiety and stress; and 4) facilitation of natural sleep in many individuals. Now, with the continuing FDA ban of L-tryptophan, everyone who previously relied upon L-tryptophan for pain control, depression, anxiety, PMS, various manic-depressive and/or obsessive-complusive disorders, and sleep problems, are either forced to use often highly addictive, expensive, and dangerous drugs like Xanax, Valium, Halcion, Dalmane, Codeine, Prozac, Anafranil, and others, or, simply suffer.

The Real Tryptophan Story

Notwithstanding the media blitz against L-tryptophan in the fall of 1989, people then aware of the benefits and decades-long safety record of L-tryptophan were immediately skeptical that L-tryptophan itself was responsible for the EMS condition.

Surely, it was believed, a contaminant in a particular batch of L-tryptophan was the culprit here. This original skepticism and belief in a contaminant have both been proved valid. Consider the following:

- An article by M. Specter in the *Washington Post*[1] stated that the Centers for Disease Control successfully traced virtually all cases of EMS to L-tryptophan manufactured by the Showa Denko company, a Japanese petrochemical firm. Moreover, past analytical work done at the CDC and the Mayo Clinic illustrated convincingly that the then-discovered contaminant (1-1'-ethylidenebis[tryptophan]) found in the Showa Denko tryptophan could be traced to tryptophan manufactured from late 1988 through early 1989.

- Recently, as reported in *Nature*,[2] a second contaminant (3-phenylamino-L-aniline) has now been identified. This particular contaminant, also found in the same EMS-implicated batches of Showa Denko tryptophan, is similar to a cooking-oil contaminant which caused the 1981 outbreak of EMS ("Toxic Oil Syndrome") in Spain.

- Interestingly, from late 1988 through early 1989 — the same period of time during which the contaminated L-tryptophan was produced — Showa Denko simultaneously altered *three separate elements* of their manufacturing process which had for decades produced safe L-tryptophan. As reported in the *New England Journal of Medicine*,[3] these production changes were 1) the partial bypass of a reverse osmosis filter, 2) a significant reduction of the amount of activated carbon used in another filtration step, and 3) the introduction of an entirely new strain of a "biotech" (genetically engineered) microorganism used in L-tryptophan fermentation. Those acquainted with Japanese industrial practices find it unbelievable, and inexplicable, that three separate production factors were changed at the same time. Such an action by Showa Denko renders all scientific manufacturing quality controls useless.

- In addition to the analysis of impurities and epidemiological investigation into the social distribution of EMS, a direct cause-and-effect relationship produced by contaminated Showa Denko L-tryptophan has been documented. As reported in the *Journal of Clinical Investigation*,[4] contaminated Showa Denko L-tryptophan caused human EMS-like conditions in scientifically controlled experiments using an animal model. This same study also revealed that administration of United States Pharmacopoeia-grade L-tryptophan (USP pure) caused no symptoms or changes whatsoever.

Despite identifying the specific company responsible for the contaminated batches of L-tryptophan which caused the EMS outbreak, the FDA has not allowed uncontaminated L-tryptophan back on the market. This is strange and highly irregular. In past instances, when contaminated foods (tuna, cheese, etc.) and over-the-counter drugs (Tylenol, Contac, etc.) were identified and corrected, uncontaminated foods and drugs were subsequently allowed back into the marketplace. Conspicuously, such has not been the case with L-tryptophan.

The current FDA position on tryptophan is that L-tryptophan *itself*, irrespective of contamination, is a dangerous substance. Gary Dykstra, chairman of the FDA diet-supplement task force, explains: "The theory that the sole reason for the EMS outbreak was a contaminant in one batch of the supplement has been challenged by scientists who claim to have found evidence that the contaminant merely exacerbated a problem that is inherent in the amino acid."[5] As reported in *Nature*, one such scientist is FDA researcher, Lori Love.[6] Ostensibly, Dr. Love's yet-unpublished work with rats will cast doubt on the safety of consuming large quantities of L-tryptophan.

Although the FDA is holding up questions of safety as justification for withholding reintroduction of tryptophan to the US marketplace, their flagrant disregard of tryptophan's impressive safety record prior to the 1989 Showa Denko EMS epidemic makes it clear to this investigator that the FDA is now moving towards regulating the production and sale of L-tryptophan as a federally controlled drug, rather than as a dietary supplement. In this FDA-sponsored reality, L-tryptophan compounds marketed by pharmaceutical companies under watchful FDA regulations will become safe for human use.

Any such arguments made by the FDA, or others, which automatically equate substance safety and FDA drug control, are both ahistorical and specious. In the United States, for example, there is ample evidence that federally regulating medicinal substances as drugs does not, in itself, assure public or product safety. The human disasters caused by the FDA-approved and regulated drugs DES, Thalidomide, and Oraflex immediately come to mind. Moreover, and directly to the point at hand, German L-tryptophan (governmentally regulated and publicly used as a drug) caused 69 cases of Showa Denko-

implicated EMS at the same time the epidemic happened in the United States.[7]

If the primary FDA goal of regulating L-tryptophan as a drug is to ensure its safety, the recurrent examples of unsafe federally regulated drugs *per se*, both domestic and abroad, should undermine arrogant bureaucratic optimism that reclassification and FDA control is the needed prescription for L-tryptophan. Only vigilant and sound manufacturing quality control can ensure the production purity and safety of L-tryptophan. As presently structured, the FDA possesses the same legal authority to protect and regulate the quality and purity of L-tryptophan as it does to protect and regulate the quality and purity of the rest of the nation's food supply. Current FDA plans for L-tryptophan drug reclassification and control are questionable.

The Pharmaceutical Connection

The ban of L-tryptophan continues. As such, other recent past events and issues which possibly impact current L-tryptophan policy are worthy of attention:

- Before the 1989 recall of L-tryptophan, sales of L-tryptophan in the United States alone were approximately 180 million dollars per year (steadily growing throughout the 1980s). The pharmaceutical industry realized none of this revenue.
- In early 1990, the FDA conducted closed-door/closed-record meetings with the Showa Denko company with regard to the EMS condition. To this day, under the umbrella of federal proprietary laws in industrial manufacturing, the FDA has released no information concerning pertinent Showa Denko manufacturing procedures. No adequate explanation has been advanced for Showa Denko's irresponsible alteration of its previously safe manufacturing practice for L-tryptophan — a change completely inconsistent with the careful, scientific standards of Japanese industrial and manufacturing activities.
- At the same time the FDA is banning L-tryptophan — the most effective serotonin producer currently known — it

grants distribution rights in the United States to the chemical antidepressant, Anafranil (as of 17 February 1990). Used as drug therapy for obsessive-compulsive disorder and depression, Anafranil has been sold outside the United States for 20 years. It is produced and marketed by the pharmaceutical company Ciba-Geigy. Anafranil is a serotonin "enhancer" — i.e., it attempts to inhibit neuronal reuptake of serotonin, to prevent nerves from reabsorbing whatever amounts of serotonin already exist in one's body, thereby enhancing serotonin. Unlike L-tryptophan, however, Anafranil does not itself produce serotonin in the human body. And, also unlike L-tryptophan, Anafranil can produce numerous adverse side effects, including tremor, dizziness, headache, insomnia, libido change, nervousness, and others.

- Prozac, another chemical antidepressant, it too just a serotonin enhancer, is currently widely prescribed. Marketed by the Eli Lilly company, Prozac's retail price is $1.60 per capsule. By 1995, sales of Prozac are expected to top $1 billion. Sadly, however, like Anafranil, Prozac can cause serious adverse side effects, including headache, nervousness, and gastric disorders. Recently, Prozac has even been implicated in several suicides and violent assaults. The FDA, of course, contests this association.

- While the FDA has banned the sale and use of non-contaminated, safe L-tryptophan in humans, the United States Department of Agriculture still sanctions the legal sale of L-tryptophan for use in animals. Safe and non-contaminated feed-grade L-tryptophan has been and continues to be used as a nutritional and bulk feed additive by the commercial hog and chicken-farming industry. As reported in the *Chemical Marketing Reporter*,[8] Heartland Lysine company — a Chicago-based, jointly owned Japanese and French business — still imports and sells feed-grade L-tryptophan in the United States. The *CMR* article, titled "Tryptophan Scare Extends To Feed Additive Market," goes on to state that the Archer Daniels Midland company will complete constructing facilities by the end of

1991 for the first-time production of L-tryptophan in the United States.

• As reported in *Advances In Therapy*,[9] USP-pure L-tryptophan was used successfully as part of an EMS-treatment regimen. In combination with other vitamins and minerals, a South Carolina psychiatrist gave USP tryptophan to 20 EMS patients who had found no relief from standard steroid therapy. Significant improvement resulted in all 20 cases.

Nutrients versus Drugs?

With regard to national health matters, the picture which emerges is perverse and Kafkaesque: often-dangerous serotonin-enhancer drugs like Prozac and Anafranil are increasing in sales at the same time that L-tryptophan, a safe serotonin-producing amino acid, is made unavailable to people, but fed to hogs and chickens. Moreover, L-tryptophan, the very substance popularly reputed as the cause of EMS, has now been shown to be a significant aid in its treatment.

As reported in *Medical Marketing and Media*,[10] neurological drugs are the ones to watch in coming years. Many of these neurological drugs, and the sales volume they generate, will be serotonin oriented. In the treatment of migraine headaches, bipolar psychological problems, depression, and eating disorders, the medical benefits of serotonin are now beginning to be fully explored, understood, and utilized. With L-tryptophan legally unavailable for human nutritional use, the pharmaceutical industry has clear sailing ahead in the competition for serotonin-enhancing drugs and future L-tryptophan compounds. Winners will reap billions of dollars in profits. An early entrant in this race, for example, is the serotonin-enhancer sumatriptan, an anti-migraine drug currently being researched by Glaxo Incorporated. Once fully approved by the FDA, sumatriptan (trade name Imitrex) will be marketed to migraine sufferers across the nation, producing untold millions in revenue.

Conclusion

For reasons outlined above, the present and continuing FDA ban of non-contaminated L-tryptophan in general, and USP-grade L-tryptophan in particular, seems unwarranted, harmful, and biased in favor of the pharmaceutical industry. It is important to remember that during the 1980s, the FDA's reputation was damaged by several scandals, including favoritism in the approval of generic drugs and the bribery of FDA officials. Have these or other FDA "problems" from the 1980s persisted into the 1990s? At least with regard to L-tryptophan — in the absence of a full, impartial, and aggressive congressional investigation into relevant Showa Denko production practices and FDA L-tryptophan policy — this question remains open.

References

1. *Washington Post*, 26 April 1990.
2. *Nature*, 9 July 1992.
3. *New England Journal of Medicine*, August 1990.
4. *Journal of Clinical Investigation*, November 1990.
5. *Food Chemical News*, 30 September 1991.
6. *Nature*, 10 October 1991.
7. James B. Roufs, Review of L-tryptophan and eosinophilia myalgia syndrome. *Journal of the American Dietetic Association* 92(7): 846, July 1992.
8. *Chemical Marketing Reporter*, 1 April 1991.
9. *Advances In Therapy*, July/August 1990.
10. *Medical Marketing and Media*, January 1990.

Editor's notes: *An earlier and different version of "The Curious Continuing Ban of L-Tryptophan: The Serotonin Connection" appeared in the* Townsend Letter for Doctors *(October 1992). This article is updated and revised, copyright © 1992, by Dean W. Manders. Correspondence to Dr. Manders should be addressed to him at: P. O. Box 20985, Piedmont, CA 94620.*

The FDA's recalls of tryptophan (first recall 17 November 1989, second recall 22 March 1992) did not initially include manufacturers of infant formulas and total parenteral nutrition (TPN) products. It wasn't until December of 1990 and the early months of 1991 that the FDA recalled Showa Denko tryptophan being used in infant formulas, injectables, and TPN formulas. During the intervening months, the FDA allowed infants, and sick and invalid patients to continue consuming contaminated tryptophan made by Showa Denko. The degree of illness and death that resulted from this bureaucratic oversight is unknown, uninvestigated, and unpublicized.

Dr. Manders briefly mentions the generic-drug scandal that took place at the FDA, but he does not mention that the FDA was later caught taking retalitory action against the drug companies who "blew the whistle" on the FDA's corruption and who cooperated in the Congressional investigation of FDA malfeasance. There have also been allegations of insider-trading of pharmaceutical stocks by FDA employees made to the US Securities and Exchange Commission. The FDA's problems really are deeper than many Americans realize.

L-Deprenyl:
An Anti-Aging Aphrodisiac?

by Steven Wm. Fowkes

Steven Fowkes is the Executive Director of the Cognitive Enhancemet Research Institute (CERI), and the Editor of Smart Drug News. *This article originally appeared in the inaugural issue of* Smart Drug News. *Deprenyl is the treatment of choice for Parkinson's disease and an up-and-coming drug for Alzheimer's disease. It is also being suggested as a general geriatric drug for people over 40-45 years of age, for which it is establishing enthusiastic grass-roots support.*

L-Deprenyl (selegiline, Eldepryl) is unique among the smart drugs. Discovered in the 1950s and researched by Dr. Jozsef Knoll since the 1960s, deprenyl is the only drug known to selectively enhance the activity of the nigrostriatal (substantia nigra) region of the brain. This brain region is exceptionally rich in dopaminergic (dopamine-using) neurons which regulate such primitive functions as motor control and sex drive. It is also implicated in the aging process and the development of Parkinson's disease.

L-Deprenyl is chemically related to phenethylamine (PEA), a substance found in chocolate and produced in higher-than-normal amounts in the brains of people who are "in love." L-Deprenyl's chemical structure is also closely related to amphetamine ("speed"), which, like PEA, is able to cross into brain neurons and trigger the release of catecholamine neuro-transmitters (norepinephrine, epinephrine and dopamine) which cause mental stimulation. Deprenyl, however, does not trigger neurotransmitter release. In this respect, deprenyl is unique among PEA derivatives.

L-deprenyl is a member of a class of drugs called mono-amine oxidase (MAO) inhibitors. MAO is a neurotransmitter biodegrading enzyme responsible for oxidizing (burning up) used neurotransmitters so that they can be excreted. MAO levels tend to rise with age. Correspondingly, monoamine neurotransmitters tend to fall with age.

MAO inhibition can correct for this age-related decrease in neurotransmitters, but when MAO is over-inhibited, mono-amines can build up to excessive levels causing neuronal hyper-stimulation — hence the "speediness" effect of amphetamines. L-Deprenyl manages to avoid this side-effect by inhibiting only a selected form of MAO.

Forms of Monoamine Oxidase

MAO enzymes are found throughout the body and come in two known types: type A (found in most body tissues, including dopaminergic neurons of the substantia nigra) and type B (predominantly found in brain glial cells which surround and support neurons).

Most MAO inhibitors are unselective, inhibiting both MAO-A and MAO-B. When MAO-A is inhibited (with amphetamines, for example), a dangerous high blood pressure reaction can occur in patients eating tyramine-containing foods (like cheese). This same reaction can occur in patients taking L-dopa for Parkinson's disease. Unlike other MAO inhibitors, L-Deprenyl inhibits only MAO-B. It does not cause the "cheese reaction" and it can be safely administered with L-dopa.

L-Deprenyl was the first selective MAO-B inhibitor to be described in the literature. Over the last 30 years, it has become the "reference standard" for MAO-B inhibition. It is still the only one in clinical use today.

Brain Function Enhancement

Deprenyl both inhibits the uptake of monoamine neuro-transmitters and potentiates the release of dopamine in nigro-striatal neurons. Deprenyl-induced enhancement of nigro-striatal function manifests in several dramatic ways. Elderly male rats treated with deprenyl regained their sexual function, maintained their learning ability longer, and lived longer than saline-treated controls (see graph next page). In man, deprenyl significantly delays the progression of Parkinson's disease.

Newly diagnosed Parkinson patients treated with L-deprenyl take longer than untreated patients for their symptoms to worsen enough to require L-dopa treatment. Advanced Parkinson patients treated with L-deprenyl plus L-dopa lived longer than those on L-dopa alone. L-Deprenyl has also improved the mental performance of Alzheimer's patients. More research with deprenyl in Alzheimer's disease is underway.

Free Radicals, Oxidation and Aging

Deprenyl's effects on nigrostriatal metabolism include not only elevated production and release of dopamine but enhanced levels of superoxide dismutase (SOD) and catalase, two enzymes which protect against oxidative damage to neuro-

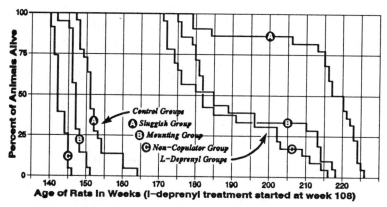

Effect of L-Deprenyl and Sex Activity on Lifespan of Rats
Two-year-old rats were classified into one of three groups by their performance on a sexual activity test. All rats exhibited diminished sexual activity by this age. Highest-performing rats were classified in the "sluggish" group, rats which mounted but did not perform intromission were classified in the "mounting" group, and rats that did not even mount were classified in the "non-copulating" group. Half of each group was treated with long-term L-deprenyl, the other half received saline. In all three groups, deprenyl-treated rats lived substantially longer. Higher-performing males lived longer than under-performing males in both the control and deprenyl groups. This suggests a strong association between the activity of dopaminergic neurons of the substantia nigra and lifespan. Dopaminergic neurons may be a focus of the aging process due to the sensitivity of dopamine to oxidizing free radicals. Deprenyl (and antioxidants) provide a clinically effective means to ameliorate premature aging (Parkinsonism) and possibly retard the aging process in normal, healthy individuals.

transmitters and neurons. In fact, it is the oxidative polymerization of L-dopa and dopamine (along with other aromatic amines and amino acids) that produces the black melanin pigment which colors the nigrostriatal (black striated) region of the brain.

The oxidation of L-dopa and dopamine produces numerous free-radical intermediates which bear close resemblances to known free-radical neurotoxins, some of which cause symptoms similar to Parkinsonism. Control of antioxidant defenses is critical to the health and vitality of dopamine-containing neurons.

The aging of striatal neurons may play a central role in the aging process. The decrease of dopamine levels with age is striking — 13% per decade after age 45. Deprenyl treatment not only corrects for this age-associated decrease, it extends mean and maximum lifespan in the process.

While dopamine levels universally decrease with age, the specific rate at which it does so varies with each individual. When dopamine falls to 30% of normal levels, Parkinsonian symptoms result. Even minor variations in dopamine decline can drastically influence the time at which Parkinsonism manifests.

Toxicity

No mutagenic (mutation-causing) or teratogenic (birth defect-causing) effects have been observed with L-deprenyl. In animal experiments, the LD-50 (lethal) dose is approximately 300-500 times greater than the dose required for complete MAO-B inhibition. Human patients have tolerated up to 60 mg of deprenyl for depression for over three weeks without difficulty. The hypertensive reaction that occurs with MAO-A inhibitors following ingestion of tyramine-containing foods (like cheese, chianti wine, beans, chicken liver) has not been observed in patients taking the standard 5-10 mg dose of deprenyl. This response is observed to some degree at the 60 mg dose.

Dosage

For Parkinsonism, recommended dosage of deprenyl is 5-10 mg daily. For the healthy population 45 and older, Dr. Knoll recommends 10-15 mg *per week*. For younger people, much smaller doses may suffice. Some people take only 1/4-1/2 tablet (1.25-2.5 mg) once a week.

L-deprenyl causes a general stimulation of mental function that is distinctly different from other catecholamine-oriented drugs (phenylalanine, tyrosine, L-dopa, and amphetamine). Most people report a mild-to-moderate anti-depressant effect, increased energy, improved feelings of well-being, substantially increased sex drive, and more assertiveness. The effect is mild in low doses and can last for several days.

As the dose of deprenyl is increased, symptoms of over-stimulation can result. People have reported feeling "over-amped," sexually overstimulated, nauseous, and even "detached" from their surroundings. When too much L-deprenyl is taken, the stimulation that it produces becomes L-dopa-like or amphetamine-like. People find it tiresome because it lasts so long.

With deprenyl, more is definitely not necessarily better. Starting with low doses and increasing gradually is the best policy.

Conclusion

L-Deprenyl is a unique drug offering selective inhibition of MAO-B, enhancement of dopamine synthesis and release, and elevation of nigrostriatal antioxidant enzymes, without the necessity for dietary restriction of tyramine foods. It selectively protects dopaminergic neurons from accelerated aging that not only leads to loss of drive, but to loss of motor control and eventually Parkinson's disease. Deprenyl is capable of simultaneously enhancing the quality of life and extending lifespan. Only time will tell whether deprenyl will make sexually active centenarians commonplace.

References

1. Knoll J, The possible mechanism of action of (-)deprenyl in Parkinson's

disease. *Journal of Neural Transmission* 43: 239-44, 1978.

2. Knoll J, Yen TT, and Dallo J, Long-lasting, true aphrodisiac effect of (-)deprenyl in sluggish old male rats. *Mod. Probl. Pharmacopsychiat.* 19: 135-53, 1983.

3. Sunderland T, *et al.* Tyramine pressor sensitivity changes during deprenyl treatment. *Psychopharmacology* 1985.

4. Tariot PN, *et al.* L-Deprenyl in Alzheimer's Disease: Preliminary evidence for behavioral change with monoamine oxidase B inhibition. *Archives of General Psychiatry* 44: 427-33, May 1987.

5. Martini E, *et al.* *Pharmacopsychiatry* 20: 256, 1987.

6. Knoll J, The striatal dopamine dependency of life span in male rats. Longevity study with (-)deprenyl. *Mechanisms of Ageing and Development* 46: 237-62, 1988.

7. Knoll J, Extension of life span of rats by long-term (-)deprenyl treatment. *Mount Sinai J Med* 55: 67-74, 1988.

8. Knoll J, The pharmacology of selegiline ((-)deprenyl). New aspects. *Acta Neurol Scand* 126: 83-91, 1989.

9. The Parkinson Study Group, Effect of deprenyl on the progression of disability in early Parkinson's disease. *The New England Journal of Medicine* 321: 1364-71, 16 November 1989.

10. Letters to the Editor on deprenyl in Parkinson's disease. *New England Journal of Medicine* 322: 1526-7, 24 May 1990.

11. Milgram NW, *et al.* Maintenance on L-deprenyl prolongs life in aged male rats. *Life Sciences* 47: 415-20, 1990.

Editor's notes: *Deprenyl is available in the United States by prescription as Eldepryl. It is also available overseas from: World Health Services, P. O. Box 20, CH-2822 Courroux, Switzerland. You can write to them for prices. A liquid form of deprenyl that is not manufactured from amphetamine and may have significantly enhanced activity is being manufactured by Discovery Experimental and Development (Mexico). A New Drug Application has been filed with the FDA by Discovery Experimental and Development (Florida) for this liquid deprenyl, but approval has been stalled. In the meantime, their liquid deprenyl is available from Mexico. Phone 619-661-0010, 619-661-1070, or 813-973-7354 to make arrangements with the factory in Mexico.*

Sources for overseas drugs are always rapidly changing. The FDA states publicly that they allow for the personal importation of overseas drugs in cases of life-threatening or seriously debilitating conditions for which satisfactory treatment is not available in the United States (see the FDA's Personal Importation Policy). But the FDA's actions do not align with their words. Tacrine, the Alzheimer's drug, has been placed on an import alert and remains there to this day. Also, six overseas companies have had an import alert placed on their shipments, regardless of their intended use. As a result, the companies shipping pharmaceuticals into the United States tend to cease business or go out of business when the FDA turns *up the heat. An up-to-date listing of companies willing to ship drugs to United States residents is available from CERI for a self-addressed-stamped envelope (or $1): CERI Source List, P. O. Box 4029-2001, Menlo Park, CA 94026-4029.*

You can subscribe to Smart Drug News *for $40/year (10 issues) (or $49 for international subscriptions). Subscriptions include both CERI's Sources Listing and their Physician Listing. Phone 415-321-CERI. VISA and MasterCard accepted.*

Does the FDA Need Smart Drugs?

by Ward Dean, MD

Dr. Ward Dean is the Medical Director of the Center for Bio-gerontology in Pensacola, Florida. A graduate of West Point, he has served as an Army Flight Surgeon and has participated in classified Delta Force operations. Dr. Dean has been actively engaged in gerontological research since 1977 and is the author of 60 articles and reviews for professional journals. He is the author of Biological Aging Measurement — Clinical Applications *(1988), co-author of* Smart Drugs & Nutrients *(1991) with John Morgenthaler, and coauthor of* The Neuroendocrine Theory of Aging and Degenerative Disease *(1992) with distinguished Russian Professor Vladimir M. Dilman, MD, PhD, DMSc.*

In February 1992, the FDA released a "Talk Paper" on smart drugs, in response to the rising popularity of the book Smart Drugs & Nutrients *(co-authored by Ward Dean and John Morgenthaler), and extensive media attention on the issue. A Talk Paper is an internal FDA document automatically released only to internal FDA offices and personel, but interested citizens and media representatives can request one from FDA spokesperson Brad Stone (Phone: 301-443-3285). The following article is Dr. Dean's reply.*

The FDA's *Talk Paper* on smart drugs is full of misinformation, distorted facts, and outright deception. The *Talk Paper* refers to smart drugs that are obtained "fraudulently through physicians' prescriptions or imported for personal use." This is clearly deceptive, as there is nothing fraudulent about obtaining an approved substance for a legitimate use if it is prescribed by a physician. Nor is there anything fraudulent in obtaining an unapproved-but-legal substance for personal use when imported in compliance with US laws (i.e., *FDA Policy on Mail Importations*, dated 20 July 1988).

The *Talk Paper* states that the "FDA is concerned about the safety of food-based products such as amino acids and vitamins." The American public would certainly benefit if the FDA spent more time on this aspect of its charter (safety of drugs and nutrients) than it does harassing citizens and nutritional supplement manufacturers and distributors. As a physician who prescribes prescription drugs as well as nutritional supplements and herbs, I can state without equivocation that I have seen many more adverse effects from prescription drugs than I have from non-prescription natural substances. My experiences are not unique, as can be seen in the table below summarizing the relative safety of drugs versus vitamins (Loomis, 1992). Loomis' report is based on data obtained from annual reports of the American Association of Poison Control Centers. Since 1983, there has been *only one* vitamin-related death (attributed to niacin, but probably more related to an underlying cardio vascular disease for which the niacin was a treatment). On the other hand, there were more than 2500 deaths due to several common categories of prescription medications during the same period.

The FDA's statement that "those [smart drugs] that are prescription drugs pose even greater risks" is misleading for several reasons. First, I'd like to ask, "greater risk than what?" (since we have already established the relative safety of nutritional supplements, above). Second, prescription drugs that are used for cognitive-enhancing purposes are among the safest

Fatalities from Prescription Drugs, Non-Prescription Drugs, and Nutrients

	Year								
	'83	'84	'85	'86	'87	'88	'89	'90	Total
Number of centers reporting	16	47	56	57	63	64	70	72	
Analgesics (pain killers)	22	53	87	82	93	118	126	134	715
Antidepressants (mood elevators)	19	57	90	100	105	135	140	159	805
Asthma Therapies	4	10	11	21	16	27	34	37	160
Cardiovascular Drugs[1]	5	18	21	50	52	65	70	79	360
Sedatives and Hypnotics[2]	11	51	62	61	48	77	78	72	460
Deaths from Amphetamines[3]	1	4	6	11	11	12	5	6	56
Deaths from all above drugs	62	193	227	325	325	434	453	487	2506
Deaths attributed to all nutrients	0	0	0	0	1[†]	0	0	1	2[†]

1. Includes blood pressure medications. 2. Includes sleeping pills and tranquilizers. 3. Includes stimulants. †The 1987 vitamin-related death report was later determined to be an error. Table adapted from Donald Loomis, *Townsend Letter for Doctors*, April 1992. Original data from the American Association of Poison Control Centers. Statistics first published in the *American Journal of Emergency Medicine*.

substances known. For example, there is no known toxic dose for Hydergine® or Nootropil® (piracetam), the two most widely prescribed cognitive-enhancing drugs in the world. Other substances such as Dilantin,® Nimodepine,® L-dopa, or selegiline (deprenyl, Eldepryl®) — which are approved for purposes other than cognitive enhancement — are used in much lower doses for cognitive-enhancing purposes than for their approved indications. Thus, potential side effects that may be caused by these relatively safe substances when used for their usual therapeutic purposes are minimized or non-existent when used for cognitive-enhancing purposes.

The FDA's statement that "the drugs are frequently imported from areas outside FDA jurisdiction and often do not meet quality-control standards commonly accepted in this country and enforced by the FDA" is misleading and pure baloney! Most of the foreign drugs that are imported for cognitive-enhancing purposes are manufactured by major international pharmaceutical companies like Sandoz, Glaxo, Pfizer, Parke-Davis, ICF, Ciba-Geigy, UCB, Riker, and others. There is no evidence that these companies use less-stringent manufacturing standards overseas than they do in the US In fact, some medications that are sold in the US by prescription are actually foreign-manufactured drugs that are repackaged with a US label!

We do agree with the FDA's statement that "there are risks in using prescription drugs without the supervision of a physician." However, *nowhere* in our book *Smart Drugs & Nutrients* do we encourage readers to take cognitive-enhancing substances without the supervision of a physician. In fact, to encourage physician supervision, we even provide the names and phone numbers of medical associations whose members are likely to be knowledgeable about cognitive-enhancing substances. We also provide complimentary copies of the book to physicians of readers of the book. On the other hand, I want to emphasize that using prescription drugs even *with* the supervision of a physician is not without significant risks (see Loomis, 1992).

The FDA's claim that there is "no adequate scientific

evidence available to show that [smart drugs] are safe and effective" is just not tenable, and indicates the FDA's lack of familiarity with the available scientific literature. *Smart Drugs & Nutrients* contains over 250 citations to the scientific literature. There is an even greater body of scientific literature which was not included due to the popular nature of the book. Interested investigators can easily access these data.

The statement in the *Talk Paper* that "even ordinary nutrients such as vitamins and amino acids can be *highly toxic*" [italics ours] is unfounded. Certainly, isolated cases of mild adverse reactions can be found to *anything* — including aspirin, and even water. However, the paucity of reported adverse reactions (despite the FDA's repeated efforts to encourage physicians to report such adverse reactions) to even "megadoses" of vitamins and amino acids confirms that they are *not* "highly toxic." Even tryptophan, which the FDA claims is toxic, isn't. Prior to several bad batches (manufactured by Showa Denko) that were imported into the United States, there had been no toxicity reported from tryptophan use — despite the fact that 14 million users took tryptophan regularly over a twenty-year period. The FDA's assertion that smart drugs and nutrients are "highly toxic" — even with tryptophan — is just an empty hysterical, claim without scientific merit.

Quite the contrary, the *Talk Paper* confirms that "no injuries" have so far been reported to the FDA by the over 100,000 estimated smart drug users in this country. However, the paper again unjustifiably implies that there is a question about the "actual identity" of cognitive-enhancing substances — despite the fact that they're generally manufactured by reputable international pharmaceutical firms, as I have pointed out.

The FDA's claim that "the popularity of smart drugs is due to ill-conceived and unfounded theories based on misconceptions about how drugs and other chemicals affect the body" is itself an *ill-conceived and unfounded statement*. For example, they claim that "one of the flawed concepts is that drugs used to help correct dysfunctional brain conditions such as epilepsy or dementia can somehow elevate normal brain function to a smarter, 'better than normal' state"— but do not explain how such a concept is allegedly flawed. We, on the other hand, cite documentation that such effects *actually occur* in normal individuals (Bonke and Nickel, 1989; Schoenthaler, 1991).

Another statement incorrectly asserts that "further misguided claims that smart drugs have anti-aging properties stem from the fact that US drug companies are conducting research to develop drugs to benefit various conditions associated with aging including Alzheimer's and Parkinson's diseases." The explanations for the anti-aging properties of several substances are, in fact, based on an understanding of their physiological and biochemical properties, results of human clinical studies, and extrapolation from lifespan studies that were conducted on animals. For example, deprenyl (Knoll, 1988), melatonin (Maestroni, et al., 1988), L-dopa (Cotzias, 1974), Dilantin (Dilman and Anisimov, 1980) and DMAE (Hochschild, 1973) have all significantly extended the lifespans of experimental animals.

Another erroneous statement is that "another *false* rationale is that mental deterioration is a deficiency disease and can be prevented" [italics ours]. Again, this criticism is without substantiation, although there are a number of excellent studies that demonstrate improvement in cognitive performance with nutritional supplementation (Shoenthaler, 1991; Bonke and Nickel, 1989).

The *Talk Paper*'s reference to the numerous news features that discussed *Smart Drugs & Nutrients* as "promotions" is misleading. These news programs were no more promotions than the news programs that have featured Dr. Kessler promoting recent FDA enforcement actions.

The *Talk Paper* substantiated its attack on *Smart Drugs & Nutrients* by citing "scientists not involved in smart drug promotions who were being interviewed in press reports [who] attribute smart drugs' reputed benefits to placebo effects or to misinterpretation of the actions of stimulant ingredients such as caffeine." Why place such credibility on unsubstantiated anecdotal reports by scientists *not* associated with smart drugs? A better approach would be to discuss the subject with the many scientists who conducted the studies which were cited in *Smart*

Drugs & Nutrients and *Smart Drug News*. Furthermore, we cite numerous studies which conclude that caffeine actually *impairs* cognitive performance, rather than enhancing it, as is commonly believed.

The FDA's claim that "None of the claims for smart drugs have been subjected to testing in controlled clinical trials" is absolutely false and demonstrates the FDA's ignorance of the scientific literature. In fact, *many* such studies have been performed, in both normal and cognitively impaired subjects.

The FDA criticizes that "most marketers and promoters of smart drugs avoid putting their claims directly on the products' labels." This is obviously because such labeling would be in violation of FDA regulations and would subject the manufacturers to even greater persecution by the agency. It is no wonder that smart-drug marketers must depend on persuasive ads and sales pitches made by word of mouth through "sales reps" and organizations. Most incredible, however, of all the deceptive misinformation in the *Talk Paper*, is the statement that "Any product, regardless of its composition, that is clearly associated with smart drug claims — is illegal and subject to seizure or other actions by the [FDA] to protect the public health." Does this mean that when sombody's grandmother advises them to eat fish because it is "brain food," that Granny can be arrested and the fish seized?

The final paragraph of the *Talk Paper* perpetuates the misconception that approved drugs can be used only for approved purposes. This is clearly in violation of the FDA's own policy which states that "accepted medical practice often includes drug use that is not reflected in approved drug labeling" (FDA Drug Bulletin).

It is clear that smart drugs are the target of the latest FDA vendetta. A review of the available world literature on the subject clearly indicates that the FDA, by its obstructionist attitudes and policies — rather than protecting the health of the American public — has become the greatest single impediment to medical progress in this country.

References

1. Bonke D, and Nickel B. Improvement of fine motoric movement control by elevated dosages of vitamin B_1, B_6 and B_{12} in target shooting. *International Journal for Vitamins and Nutrition*: Research Supplement 30: 198-204, 1989.

2. Cotzias GC, Miller ST, Tang LC, Papavasilou PS, and Wang YY. Prolongation of the life-span in mice adapted to large amounts of L-dopa. *Proceedings of the National Academy of Sciences* USA 71: 2466-69, 1974.

3. Cotzias GC, Miller ST, Tang LC, Papavasilou PS, and Wang YY. Levodopa, fertility and longevity. *Science* 196: 549-51, 1977.

4. Dilman VM, and Anisimov VN. Effect of treatment with phenformin, diphenylhydantoin and L-dopa on the lifespan and tumor incidence in C3H/Sn mice. *Gerontology* 26: 241-45, 1980.

5. FDA Drug Bulletin, Washington, DC.

6. Hochschild R. Effect of dimethylaminoethanol [DMAE] on the life span of senile male A/J mice. *Experimental Gerontology* 8: 185-91, 1973.

7. Knoll J. Extension of lifespan of rats by long-term deprenyl treatment. *Mount Sinai Journal of Medicine* 55: 67-74, 1988.

8. Loomis D. Which is safer: Drugs or vitamins? *Townsend Letter for Doctors* 219: April 1992.

9. Schoenthaler S. Diet and IQ. *Nature* 352: 292, 1991.

Editor's notes: *Dr. Dean has served on the Board of Directors of the American Aging Association, and is a member of the Gerontological Society of America and the American Geriatrics Society. He is Medical Editor for* Smart Drug News, *Book Review Editor for* Experimental Gerontology, *and is on the editorial boards of* The Romanian Journal of Gerontology and Geriatrics, *the* Journal of Applied Nutrition *and* The Professional's Journal of Sports Fitness.

Biological Aging Measurement – Clinical Applications *and* The Neuroendocrine Theory of Aging and Degenerative Disease *are available from the Center for Bio-gerontology, P. O. Box 11097, Pensacola, FL 32524.*

Smart Drugs & Nutrients *and* Smart Drug News *are available from CERI, P. O. Box 4029-2001, Menlo Park, CA 94026-4029. Copies of* Smart Drugs & Nutrients *are available for $12.95 (plus CA sales tax and $3 shipping and handling). One year (10 issues) of* Smart Drug News *is $40 (or $49 for international subscriptions). Phone 415-321-CERI. VISA and MasterCard accepted.*

The FDA's Brain

The Wall Street Journal, **Wednesday, April 8, 1992.**

If David Kessler's wife ever rips her carotid artery, we hope it doesn't happen in Portland, Oregon. Because under the bureaucratic mind-set of her husband's Food and Drug Administration, Portland may not have the means to save her life.

That at least is one way to read the posterior-covering now going on at Commissioner Kessler's FDA over a device known as the detachable silicone balloon. A week ago we wrote about the uproar among US neurosurgeons after the FDA had pulled from the market this lifesaving treatment (widely available outside the US) to occlude aneurysms or bleeding blood vessels in the brain. Aroused by this bad publicity, the FDA is now scrambling to solve its public-relations problem while ignoring its deeper regulatory sickness.

Dr. Kessler, who seems to drag his agency from one astounding enforcement event to another, has dispatched his minions to assure doctors that the balloons will be available to some of them on an emergency basis. What this means is that at least some patients won't die or go blind while the FDA figures out how to dodge bad press. Other patients may not be so lucky. And of course the FDA's war against the maker of the balloons will continue until the agency wins.

Specifically, the FDA now says balloons can be made available to only 25 US sites, and then only on an as needed basis. And doctors must return their stock of balloons to their maker, Interventional Therapeutics Corp. (ITC), of South San Francisco. Then, if you're a patient at one of the lucky 25 sites, your doctor has to certify that you're in a helluva fix, that no other alternative treatment is available, and that a "review board" at your institution is supervising the surgery "protocol." Then, and only then, can your doctor request that ITC Fed-Ex a balloon overnight and save your life. Dr. Barnwell also made the mistake of settling in Portland, which under the FDA rules probably won't be one of the 25 sites. Trained under the man who has pioneered "ballooning," Dr. Grant Hieshima at the Univer- sity of California at San Francisco, Dr. Barnwell is the only "dedicated trained neuro-interventionist" in the state of Oregon. "That was my whole purpose in coming up here," he says.

Jane Henney, FDA deputy commissioner, says the agency "wants to be helpful," but has to be this strict because "we have problems" with "many of the practices" of the maker of the balloons, ITC. She claims ITC violated the terms of its clinical trial, in particular by distributing at least 400 more balloons than the 200 the FDA had allowed. This is a perfect statement of the FDA problem: By helping doctors help more patients, ITC ran afoul of the FDA "process."

The FDA's view of ITC as some nasty renegade also doesn't square with the testimony of doctors who've used its product for years. "I tell the people from the FDA, 'I know you live in the shadow of thalidomide, but ITC aren't bad people,'" says Dr. Thomas Masaryk, a neuroradiologist at the Cleveland Clinic. "The FDA has never been very good at keeping ITC informed, and ITC has just used its conscience" in providing the balloons to doctors.

In any event, the FDA clearly won't rest now until it can prove that ITC has violated some rule or another and shove the company down the drain. Otherwise, Dr. Kessler would have to admit the FDA is wrong and is costing lives. ITC, a tiny company founded by two engineers, has already had to hire a Beltway lawyer and declines to take its case to the public, lest it inspire even greater FDA spite. The FDA now refuses to accept the results of the earlier clinical trial, despite the testimony of doctors, and plans to take a new trial completely out of ITC's hands.

The maze won't do much to help emergency trauma cases, of course, or surprises in surgery. Nick Hopkins, chairman of neurosurgery at the State University of New York at Buffalo, is grateful to have some balloons available but adds, "If I'm in the middle of someone's noggin and find out I have the wrong size balloon, I can't send Federal Express to get one." Stan Barnwell, a neurosurgeon at Oregon Health Services University in Portland, adds, "What occurs in many cases like this is that you have about five minutes to block the artery."

Just Monday night, Dr. Barnwell treated an 18-year-old after a car crash and "while the boy would have probably died anyway, I would love to have had a balloon." Thanks to the FDA, he didn't. Only two months ago, Dr. Barnwell wanted a balloon to treat an elderly patient but had to settle for a coil that is riskier because it can induce small blood clots that can cause stroke. The elderly patient indeed had a stroke.

Meanwhile, in a nearby letter, the FDA's overlord himself, Rep. John Dingell of the House Energy and Commerce Committee, objects that we linked him to the balloon fiasco. His letter proves our point. We certainly did read in our news pages how FDA official James Benson was beaten over the head by Mr. Dingell until he too promised to be an enforcement zealot. FDA bureaucrats who watch one of their colleagues held up to ridicule in print and in public for being too evenhanded aren't likely to conclude that they're supposed to give the ITCs of the world even treatment. When John Dingell barks, the dogs run off to find someone to bite.

The case of the silicone balloon is, alas, a study in how Washington now works, a study in how process matters more than patients at David Kessler's FDA.

Editor's note: *Reprinted from* The Wall Street Journal *with permission, copyright © 1992, all rights reserved.*

The Strange Case of Dr. Kessler

A letter to the Editor of *The Wall Street Journal*

This letter to the editor was written by William Summers, MD (Alzheimer's Rights Alliance), James Driscoll, PhD (Vice President, Direct Action for Treatment Access), and Beverly Zakarian (President, Cancer Patients Action Alliance).

David Kessler's tenure as FDA commissioner began with high hopes. He promised faster drug approval, responsiveness to people with life-threatening diseases, and a new vision. What Dr. Kessler has delivered, however, is very different.

Instead of faster drug approval, AIDS patients got a lethal 14-month delay in reviewing AZT/ddC combination therapy. There were more stalls on cancer drugs and a stubborn impasse on THA [tacrine] for Alzheimer's patients. Instead of judicious reforms, Dr. Kessler gave us headline-grabbing seizures of orange juice and spaghetti sauce. The enforcement of FDA regulations for underground drugs for AIDS and Alzheimer's was shockingly discriminatory.

Let's take a closer look:

AIDS

In December 1990, the San Francisco Consortium of AIDS Physicians and the American Foundation for AIDS Research (AMFAR) petitioned the new FDA commissioner. Their petition asked for immediate review of two promising AIDS treatments, ddI and AZT/ddC combination therapy, and an approval decision by March 1, 1991. As a sop to AIDS activists who supported Dr. Kessler, ddI was approved in October 1991, after a six-month delay. AZT/ddC combination therapy was recommended for approval early in April by the FDA Advisory Board, but actual approval languishes like a desert mirage in the distance.

The superior efficacy of AZT/ddC combination therapy was evident at the time of the petition. It promises a major

AIDS treatment advance over AZT: up to three years' added survival, compared with only one year's added survival with AZT alone. Those additional years could enable thousands to live long enough to benefit from the next generation of treatments. AZT/ddC should have been approved when the San Francisco Consortium and AMFAR asked. It is now one year later. The person who had the undeniable authority to avert that deadly and shameful year of delay was Commissioner Kessler.

Cancer

As bad as Dr. Kessler's record is on AIDS, it's worse on cancer. Last summer he cracked down on promotion of cancer drugs for uses outside their labeled indications. This was a very harmful decision. More than half of all current cancer treatments involve off-label usage. Doctors depend on pharmaceutical companies to educate them about off-label usage. Without such continuing medical education paid for by the drug industry, doctors fall behind the state of the art. These considerations were lost on Dr. Kessler, for whom the bottom line is a headline, and the fastest route to the front page is an enforcement campaign.

Who demanded Dr. Kessler's new enforcement campaign? Not cancer patients — they are alarmed about it. The crackdown on off-label usage makes cancer doctors afraid to prescribe combinations of drugs that patients desperately need. Insurance companies are now refusing to reimburse. Regulating off-label usage was not the administration's idea. To the contrary, Vice President Dan Quayle's Council on Competitiveness opposes it as more regulation for regulation's sake. Not even Congress has the stomach for dumping new regulatory burdens on cancer patients.

The demand to regulate off-label usage came from the FDA's bureaucratic empire builders who found an eager champion in Dr. Kessler.

Alzheimer's Disease

Clinical trials in the US, Sweden and Britain show that the drug THA improves about one-third of the Alzheimer patients who suffer this otherwise untreatable affliction. THA also alleviates the suffering for their families. This wasn't good enough for Dr. Kessler. He chose instead to "protect" any patients who might experience minor, reversible liver mal- functions with THA. By keeping THA on import alert, Dr. Kessler is driving patients' families into the crime of smuggling.

If George Bush wants credibility with AIDS and cancer patients and the families of Alzheimer's victims; if he wants business to believe his promise to cut regulatory burdens; if he expects the electorate to trust him with our health-care crisis, then he needs to acknowledge a mistake: his appointment of Dr. Kessler. Mr. Bush should then appoint a commissioner truly committed to rapid drug approval and with the courage to overhaul the FDA.

William Summers, M.D.
Alzheimer's Rights Alliance
James Driscoll, Ph.D.
Vice President
Direct Action for Treatment Access
Beverly Zakarian
President
Cancer Patients Action Alliance

Editor's note: *Reprinted with permission from the authors and* The Wall Street Journal, *copyright © 1992 by* The Wall Street Journal. *All rights reserved. Originally printed in the Western Edition, May 12, 1992.*

Alzheimer's Rights Alliance, founded by Dr. William Summers, is dedicated to speeding the approval of drugs for Alzheimer's disease. They recently organized a Washington, DC demonstration against the FDA's failure to approve Tacrine. Write to them at: 624 West Duarte Road, Suite 101, Arcadia, CA 91007, or phone 818-445-6196.

Direct Action for Treatment Access *(DATA) is a non-profit chapter of the PATH Foundation founded by AIDS activists to advocate for access to life-saving therapies. Jim Driscoll, DATA Vice President in charge of politics and policy, was an author of the "Access to Life-Saving Therapies Act," sponsored by Representative Tom Campbell (R-CA). DATA, P. O.*

Box 60391, Palo Alto, CA 94306.   Phone: 415-323-6051.   FAX: 415-323-3864.   Contributions are tax deductible.

Cancer Patients Action Alliance *(CanAct) is a cancer-patient advocacy group working closely with the FDA on cancer-treatment issues. CanAct, 26 College Place, Brooklyn, NY 11201. Phone: 718-522-4607.*

Snake Oil Quackery

by Steven Wm. Fowkes

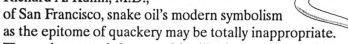

According to
Richard A. Kunin, M.D.,
of San Francisco, snake oil's modern symbolism
as the epitome of quackery may be totally inappropriate.
The snake not only has a multi-millenium tradition within the
medical profession, it is part of the medical emblem still in use
today — snakes encircling the staff of life. Over the last
hundred years, the term snake oil has come to represent the
best example of a worthless cure. Chemical analysis of snake oil
samples, however, reveals that some have significant levels of
polyunsaturated fats which serve as precursors to anti-inflam-
matory prostaglandin hormones. Chinese commercial snake oil
contained almost 20% EPA (eicosapentaenoic acid).

Dr. Kunin speculated that cold-blooded reptiles would
require higher-than-normal levels of unsaturated fats to maintain flexibility during the cold temperatures of the early
morning. Fat profiles varied considerably. The American black
rattlesnake had over 4% EPA and almost no DHA (docosa-
hexaenoic acid). Red rattlesnake oil was low in EPA (less than
1%) but high in DHA (over 5%). Chinese snake oil and red
rattlesnake oil were low in GLA (gamma-linolenic acid) and
DGLA (dihomo-gamma-linolenic acid) while black rattlesnake
oil contained 3.5% total GLA plus DGLA. Arachidonic acid,
which can produce the inflammatory prostaglandin PGE_2, was
highest in red rattlesnake oil (over 12%), median in black
rattlesnake oil (under 5%), and lowest in Chinese snake oil
(under 2.5%).

The branding of snake oil as quackery may have been
premature. Even based on the likelihood of rancidity in the
oxidation-sensitive polyunsaturate snake-oil, laws against the
marketing of all snake oils unscientifically discriminate against

those vendors who do know to properly handle and preserve the essential fatty acids and those consumers who would have benefitted had the quality product been available.

Should pork be outlawed because of a high incidence of *trichina* larvae (a nematode parasite causing trichinosis) in some pig ranchers stock? Or how about raw milk because of the small incidence of *salmonella* (a bacteria causing food poisoning)? And what about eggs and homogenized milk which also carry *salmonella*, although at an even smaller incidence?

Hysterical quack-bashing largely creates laws which fail to protect products which are beneficial. By not discriminating between products which actually harm people and those which are worthless or, more accurately, those which *might* be worthless, potentially effective treatments are legislated into quackery. One obvious solution is to require proof of harm before action can be taken against products or therapies. Of course, laws against fraud and misrepresentation have been on the books for a lot longer than anybody currently alive on this planet. Fraud laws have long been available to do battle with quacks.

Quack-bashers don't like to have to resort to fraud laws because it makes quacks (translation: products, treatments and therapists) *innocent until proven guilty*. They would rather regulate quackery out of existence by assuming worthlessness (and danger to the public) and then demanding proof of efficacy (and safety). It is much easier when quacks are guilty until proven innocent.

Editor's note: *This article originally appeared as an editorial in the June 1990 issue of Forefront — Health Investigations, of which Steven Fowkes is the editor and publisher. For subscription information, write to: P. O. Box 60637, Palo Alto, CA 94306, or phone 415-949-0919 (FAX: 415-323-3864).*

The snake-oil analyses of Richard A. Kunin, M.D., were originally published in the Western Journal of Medicine 151: 208, 1989. Dr. Kunin is a psychiatrist with a major interest in orthomolecular treatments. His office is at 2698 Pacific Avenue, San Francisco, CA 94115. Phone number: 415-346-2500.

POWs: Poisonings of War

Chemical Exposures in Operation Desert Storm Have Led to Illness Among Soldiers

by Major Richard H. Haines (Reserve)

Richard Haines is a US Army Reserve Major with 20 years experience as a soldier and reservist of the AG branch. He is a political science graduate from Michigan State and has an MBA from Butler. As a civilian he owns and operates a small estate planning business in southern Indiana. Major Haines did not serve in the Gulf but became concerned when he saw a number of his compatriots falling ill with an unexplained disease.

When I first met Joe he was suffering from a variety of unexplained symptoms: hair falling out, extreme weakness and fatigue, joint pains, and sleeping problems (including nightmares). Joe had been a combat-support soldier in Operation Desert Storm and shortly thereafter fell ill. He had been through everything the military medical system had to offer him, without result. They had no diagnosis for his condition and no treatment. Eventually, the military doctors told him it was just stress—it was all in his head—and they referred him to a psychiatrist. Then they proceeded to kick him out of the service with an unfavorable medical-board evaluation.

That might have been the end of medical support for Joe, and the beginning of a lifetime of suffering, had not hundreds of other Desert Storm troops come down with similar conditions. I am not a doctor and it was not my assigned duty to be looking into this problem but the plight of these soldiers was too much for me to ignore. I started doing a little research on my own time.

I first noticed that most of the sick soldiers were from quartermaster fuel companies. I had been a fuel officer in the past and had observed first-hand the inevitable spills, sprays, and exposures of handling fuel tactically under expedient conditions. I also had a bit of background in orthomolecular nutrition and had heard of environmental illness, a not-so-rare condition in which a person's immune system is undermined and they start reacting to a lot of very common things such as automobile exhaust, natural gas, household bleach, or chemicals used in food processing. Environmental illness can be caused by exposure to a toxic substance beyond a particular individual's ability to metabolize and eliminate the substance naturally. This seems to alter the immune system such that the individual becomes extremely sensitive thereafter to even tiny amounts of that chemical and, usually, other related chemicals. Normally, only a small percentage of those exposed are affected. This is because everyone's capacity to handle and metabolize toxic substances varies. In addition, some chemicals are more toxic than others.

I wrote a letter to my superiors suggesting that these soldiers were getting sick with multiple-chemical-sensitivity syndrome which was triggered by chronic exposures to petro-chemicals that went beyond their capacity for detoxification. I assumed that my superiors would approach this issue with the same sincere attitude that I did, and began an investigation. Instead, I got a polite brush off. I was appalled at the business-as-usual mentality regarding what appeared to be a grave and deteriorating condition affecting hundreds of soldiers.

I was very concerned about the inadequacy of the medical treatment being given to these sick soldiers. Their physicals were hurried and cursory. Low red-blood-cell counts were noted, but discounted. Lab results repeatedly showed abnormal liver function, but again, they were discounted. To their credit, a study was ordered by the 123rd Army Reserve Command but it was superficial, lacking any medical insight or epidemiological sophistication. Some soldiers pleaded with the military doctors to consider their exposures to high-dose, lead-containing petrochemicals, but their personal accounts fell on deaf ears.

Finally, in September 1992, three "environmental units" were established, but only one pursued medical expertise in environmental medicine. Several soldiers tested positive for petrochemical contamination but, as of this writing, no treatment has been offered. Finally, at my urging, several of these soldiers began to turn to alternative medicine.

Meanwhile, I assembled a database of all the afflicted Desert Storm soldiers I could locate. I included the number and type of chemical exposures, and any and all symptoms they experienced. This database started with 15-20 soldiers. Nine months later, it had grown to over 150, all of whom received periodic medical and technical updates (the November mailing consisted of over 30 pages). My current estimate is that over 1000 soldiers may be afflicted with this syndrome. The greatest uncertainty in determining the exact number is in the active-duty troops: many of these soldiers are younger, more easily intimidated, and have been told by commanders to keep quiet about being sick. The problem has been reported to be wreaking havoc with morale within the lower ranks of our major combat divisions.

I also began speaking with physicians who specialize in environmental illnesses including Dr. William Rea of Dallas, Texas and Dr. John Boyles of Centerville, Ohio. Talking with these doctors confirmed many of my findings. In their clinical opinion, the syndrome I described was classic environmental illness (EI). I began sending some of these Desert Storm soldiers to work with Drs. Rea and Boyles. Other physicians also volunteered their help.

Environmental physicians are routinely harassed by the medical system and have to fight a constant battle against orthodoxy to do what they think is state-of-the-art medicine. EI is not only unknown (or ignored) by the military medical system but is generally unaccepted by the AMA and the whole of traditional American medicine. In my quest to help these soldiers, I have come to regard Drs. Rea and Boyles as unsung heroes of the Gulf crisis.

Dr. Rea and Dr. Boyles were able to diagnose and begin treatment immediately. The treatments consisted of allergy desensitization, high-dose nutritional supplementation, enhancement of detoxification, and avoidance of the offending chemicals. This last intervention can be quite tricky since chemicals like automobile exhaust are ubiquitous. In some cases it was necessary to put soldiers on severely restricted diets, install air filters in their houses and cars, change their jobs, or even have them move out of homes with gas appliances and into all-electric housing.

The sick soldiers have begun to get better. Not all at once, for EI from such inordinate exposures as these soldiers received is something that goes away only slowly even with the most conscientious attention and dedicated treatment. But they are receiving effective treatment for the first time since their return from the Gulf.

The availability of treatment for EI patients is currently tenuous at best. The FDA, state licensing boards, and the medical establishment are at war with alternative medicine. The treatment of EI is considered alternative simply because the medical establishment does not yet recognize the validity of the diagnosis. This is a catch 22 of the most obvious kind. If the FDA and mainstream medicine are not forced to open up to alternative medicine, then fundamental medical progress will be needlessly slowed.

I personally feel that unnecessary regulation of medical practice by these bureaucracies is the most conspicuous cause of the current American health-care crisis. Millions of dollars have been spent by the military to try to help these soldiers — all a total failure. Why? Because of ignorance and an unwillingness to listen to medical people that offer a solution that is a little different (ie. innovative). If we are not willing to take care of our own soldiers in a fight against a tyrant like Saddam, then maybe we shouldn't be intervening in world conflicts at all.

Editor's Note: *If you are interested in a newsletter useful to: sick soldiers and their family members, media representatives, anybody with EI, or the general public, call Richard Haines at 812-948-9366. Physicians knowledgeable about chemical sensitivity can be referred from the American Academy of Environmental Medicine (AAEM) at 303-622-9755.*

A Call for a Moratorium on Dental Amalgams

by Murlene Brake

Murlene Brake is the President of DAMS (Dental Amalgam Mercury Syndrome), a grassroots, non-profit organization dedicated to educating the public about the health hazards associated with chronic exposure to mercury-containing silver amalgam dental fillings. DAMS was founded by patients experiencing drastic adverse health reactions from their amalgam fillings, reactions denied by the ADA. DAMS is affiliated with the International Academy of Oral Medicine, The Foundation for Toxic Free Dentistry, the Environmental Dental Association and the Toxic Elements Research Foundation. DAMS is also a petitioner in a Writ of Mandamus asking the federal courts to force the FDA to issue printed warnings about the mercury content of amalgam mixtures. They are also circulating a petition to the Secretary of Health and Human Services to ban mercury from further use in dentistry. For more information, get in touch with DAMS.

Published medical research has shown that mercury-laden dental fillings may be poisoning you. But the American Dental Association (ADA) refuses to support any type of government-imposed moratorium on the use of amalgam, pending scientific proof of its safety.

Why does the ADA actively lobby against informed consent?

Informed consent would require dentists to inform their patients that "silver" amalgam fillings contain approximately 50% mercury by weight and that other biocompatible dental filling materials are available. The ADA has gone to considerable length and expense to oppose and defeat informed-consent legislation in several states.

Why does the ADA, a trade union, ignore scientific research?

During 1990 and 1991, the results of animal studies done at the University of Calgary Medical School were published. These studies demonstrated that after placement of "silver" amalgam dental fillings in the teeth of animals, mercury from these fillings passed the placental barrier and accumulated in the fetus within 48 hours; and accumulations of mercury in the kidneys caused a 50% impairment of kidney function within 30 days. Further, a University of Georgia study revealed mercury-induced resistance to antibiotics after 16 small occlusal mercury fillings were placed in the teeth of monkeys. Antibiotic resistance is becoming a major medical problem in the treatment of many human diseases. Although all of the studies were published in peer-reviewed medical journals, the ADA immediately claimed the studies were flawed and invalid.

Also in 1991, the results of autopsy studies by medical researchers at the University of Kentucky revealed strikingly high levels of mercury in the brains of individuals who had died of Alzheimer's Disease. The data, together with other laboratory data, have led these researchers to conclude that mercury must be considered as a probable cause of Alzheimer's Disease and that the most likely source for the mercury in the brains of Alzheimer victims is dental amalgam fillings. The University of Kentucky has just obtained a major federal grant to study the connection of amalgam dental filings to Alzheimer's Disease.

Who or what gives the ADA the right to make risk assessments for the public?

The ADA, without any supporting epidemiological data, has announced that only about 1% of the American public are hypersensitive to amalgam dental fillings. The ADA has not instituted any studies to validate the 1% figure, nor have they provided dentists with any means to determine who is, or isn't, in the 1%. They have simply decided to risk the health and well-being of approximately 2 million people (children included) without the benefit of Informed Consent.

Why does the ADA ignore the ever-mounting clinical and scientific evidence that mercury from amalgams causes or exacerbates health problems?

Thousands upon thousands of people have decided to take the gamble in having their amalgams removed and replaced with non-toxic, biocompatible dental filling materials — and won. They experienced noticable health improvement or a recovery from their medical problems. If that is a placebo effect, as the ADA claims, then it is a most powerful placebo.

Why has the ADA declared that the removal of amalgam restorations is improper and unethical?

The ADA's Code of Ethics states that it is unethical to remove amalgams from the non-allergic patient, yet the ADA has not instituted methods of identifying "allergic" patients. In addition, it is not improper or unethical to remove an amalgam filling and replace it with a new amalgam filling, or to recommend replacement of amalgams for cosmetic reasons.

Why and how can the ADA institute campaigns that result in governmental agencies such as the Food and Drug Administration, the National Institutes of Health, and the National Institute of Dental Research ignoring their own regulations and mandates, and issue statements that mercury amalgams are safe in the face of overwhelming scientific, clinical, and anecdotal evidence?

In 1976, when the Medical Device Amendment to the Federal Food, Drug, and Cosmetic Act was enacted, the components of amalgams were classified and amalgam should have been classified as a Class III device, which would require amalgam manufacturers to produce scientific evidence that amalgam was safe to place in humans. In 1991, an FDA Dental Products Panel of the Medical Devices Advisory Committee Panel ignored the following facts: (1) amalgam *has never been approved* by the FDA as a dental device; (2) *no evidence exists* indicating that amalgam is safe; and (3) scientific, clinical and anecdotal evidence indicating that amalgam is unsafe *does exist.*

Then, in August of 1991, the NIH Technology Assessment Conference ignored their own mandate to consider *only scientific evidence* and issued a statement to the media that amalgam is safe. The statement was suspiciously similar to the ADA's statement.

Why will the ADA spend unprecedented amounts of money to block county requirements that dental offices obtain an industrial waste-water discharge permit for mercury?

In 1984, the Pima County (Arizona) Waste Water Management Department initiated requirements that dental offices obtain an industrial waste-water discharge permit for mercury. The county set the mercury discharge limit at 0.05 milligrams per liter and began to conduct random tests of dental offices. One Tucson dentist received a notice from the waste-water department that his office had exceeded the mercury limits on two dates and that, by federal law, he could be fined $25,000 for each of those two days. The ADA went into action and pressured the waste-water board into suspending the permit regulation for one year until further scientific research can be conducted by Pima County with the cooperation of the state and local dental associations. The ADA contends that the amount of mercury discharged from dental offices is negligible and that mercury does not leach from scrap amalgam during conventional biological waste-water treatment. The ADA announced in the January 1992 issue of the *ADA News* that they are prepared to do the same in other communities that begin to look at the same environmental issues.

Why does the ADA fight so vigorously to continue to use amalgam?

There are many dental materials available that are biocompatible and make effective, long-lasting restorations. Amalgam is the only dental material that requires being handled as a toxic hazard *before and after* it is implanted in teeth. Scrap amalgam must be disposed of according to hazardous materials regulations and the EPA has fined several dentists for improperly disposing of amalgam and contamination of landfills.   One average-size dental mercury filling contains enough mercury to exceed the EPA adult intake standard for non-dietary mercury for *over 100 years*. In addition, the World Health Organization has concluded that the largest estimated average daily intake and retention of mercury and mercury compounds in the general population, not occupationally exposed, is from *dental amalgams*, not from food or air.

How can the ADA declare that the amount of mercury vapor released from dental mercury fillings is minuscule and cannot be considered clinically significant?

Mercury toxicology experts of the World Health Organization have stated that *no amount of exposure to mercury vapor* can be considered totally harmless. It is obvious that the ADA has agendas other than safeguarding the public's health and the earth's environment.

In this time of ever-increasing medical costs that are threatening to bankrupt our country, it should be considered criminal negligence for anyone in any organization to continue to ignore the overwhelming scientific evidence indicating mercury from "silver" amalgam dental fillings is a possible cause of a variety of disease states that can only increase our health care costs. Suitable replacement dental materials are available. There is no longer any justification for the continued implantation of a documented poison in the teeth of humans.

The disregard for our environment adversely affects us all. We must insist upon measures to protect the health and well-being of this and future generations, even if this price is a temporary economic loss. We must safeguard the health and well-being of our unborn babies. Our waterways and water sources must be protected from further mercury contamination.

The following organizations challenge the ADA to call for and support a moratorium on the use of amalgam as a dental restorative, until science proves they are safe to use in human beings:

- DAMS (Dental Amalgam Mercury Syndrome), a victim support group
- The International Academy of Oral Medicine and Toxicology
- The Environmental Dental Association
- The Foundation for Toxic-Free Dentistry
- Toxic Element Research Foundation

Make your views known on this subject. Write to your state and federal representatives. To reach us, write DAMS, 725-9 Tramway Lane N.E., Albuquerque, NM 87122. Phone: 505-291-8239.

Editor's notes: *In addition to coordinating petition efforts, DAMS also offers a referral listing of mercury-free dental practitioners and other mercury-related literature.*

The mercury issue is highly controversial, and has been so for over a century. Originally introduced as a cheap substitute for gold for the poor, it was fiercely contested by the American Society of Dental Surgeons (ASDS) which called it quackery and enforced a vigorous anti-mercury covenant that involved ostracizing dentists caught using amalgam. Economics eventually won out, the ASDS folded to be replaced by the ADA, and the situation reversed itself. Amalgam became orthodoxy and critics became quacks. Dentists refusing to use amalgam were ostracized, and dentists who removed perfectly functional amalgam fillings were persecuted. Lately, the scientific basis of mercury toxicity, especially with respect to the central nervous system and the developing fetus, has been carefully researched, with alarming findings. A complete reappraisal of amalgam policy would be prudent. You will probably hear more about this subject in the near future.

NCIH and Other Groups Advocating Health Freedom

by Claire A. Farr

Claire A. Farr is the President of the National Council for Improved Health (NCIH) and President and founder of Klaire Laboratories, Inc., a manufacturer of nutritional supplements which are well-tolerated by even the most sensitive individuals. People who see Claire today, radiating with life and energy, would not guess that a long-term, serious environmental illness drove her to make the first starch- and sugar-free supplements available. Claire is truly dedicated to the fields of nutritional, bio-ecologic and orthomolecular medicine.

On August 10th, 1990, a group of nutritional manufacturers met to find a way to return safe, non-contaminated L-tryptophan to the market. On August 9th, I had been alerted to the existence of the horrendous Asset Seizure law (Bergeson's S 2872). This bill had passed both California state houses and was ready to go through the last committee meeting, then on to the Governor for signature.

The bill stated that if anyone would prescribe, recommend, give away or intimate the use of any product or instrument for the treatment or cure of cancer other than those product(s) authorized by the FDA, there would be immediate seizure of the product(s) and all assets of the parties involved. Immediately, the importance of opposing this bill was realized, and NCIH was formed about one hour before Bergeson's committee meeting. Clinton and Bonnie Miller were hired as our registered lobbyists, and they immediately formally protested against this bill for NCIH. The Millers had attained national recognition from their work with the successful passage of the Proxmire Amendments in 1976.

After lodging the protest, Mr. Miller was informed that the committee meeting was postponed. The following Monday we were informed that the bill had been killed and that NCIH was instrumental in this action.

We quickly realized that in order to get uncontaminated L-tryptophan back into the market, much lobbying had to be done. Almost weekly, new threatening bills were being introduced on state and Federal levels. Our freedom of choice was disappearing rapidly.

In just two years' time we have become one of the foremost lobbying organizations with a dedicated national membership. If you, too, are "fed up" with bureaucratic nonsense, come join us. Don't sit back and watch your freedoms disappear!!! Join the health freedom advocacy groups that are listed below:

Citizens Alliance for Progressive Health Awareness (CAPHA)
PO Box 394, Wayne, PA 19087   **215-640-2788**
A grassroots organization, send SASE for more information.

Citizens for Health (CFH)   **206-922-2457**
PO Box 368, Tacoma, WA 98401   **FAX: 206-922-7583**
Non-profit citizens organization dedicated to promoting good health.

Council for Responsible Nutrition (CRN)   **FAX: 202-872-9594**
1300 19th Street NW, #310, Washington, DC 20036   **202-872-1488**
A research organization doing work in the field of vitamins, minerals, amino acids and nutrients.

Foundation for the Advancement of Innovative Medicine (FAIM)
2 Executive Blvd., Suite 201, Sussern, NY 10901   **914-368-9797**
An educational non-profit New York group dedicated to health freedom.

Health Forum (HF)   **801-224-2987**
PO Box 1973, Provo, UT 84603   **FAX: 801-221-0663**
A grassroots lobbying organization for professionals and consumers alike.

National Council for Improved Health (NCIH)   **619-471-5090**
1555 West Seminole, San Marcos, CA 92069
A grassroots organization of manufacturers, retailers and health professionals.

National Health Federation   **818-357-2181**
P. O. Box 688, Monrovia, CA 91017   **FAX: 818-303-0642**

National Nutritional Food Association (NNFA)   **714-966-6632**
150 Paularino, Suite 285, Costa Mesa, CA 92626 **FAX: 714-641-7005**
An association of manufacturers and retailers lobbying for health freedom and education.

Natural Health Care Alliance   **FAX: 415-731-3850**
1348 La Playa Avenue #2, San Francisco, CA 94122   **415-731-8115**
An organization dedicated to responsible natural health care.

New England Health Freedom Coalition   **413-586-3800**
c/o Cornucopia Foods, 150 Main, Northampton, MA 01060
An association of retailers and consumers focusing on the New England area.

Nutritional Health Alliance (NHA)   **800-226-4642**
PO Box 267, Farmingdale, NY 11735
One of the largest organizations with grassroots, health professionals, manufacturers and retailers working to ensure health freedom.

People for Reason in Science and Medicine (PRISM)   **818-345-9654**
PO Box 1305, Woodland Hills, CA 91365
A non-profit health and environmental organization concerned with health freedom and education.

So What's a Person to Do?

by Monica Miller

Monica Miller is a "pissed-off" patient who set down her paint brushes to defend her family doctor when he was investigated by the state of New York for practicing homeopathy. One thing having led to another, she is now a professional lobbyist whose clients include the Foundation for the Advancement of Innovative Medicine, for issues regarding the medical professions in New York state, and the Nutritional Health Alliance, for issues regarding dietary supplements and the FDA. She still paints, too.

You have read the articles, newsletters, and opinion pieces. You have talked to your doctor, or friend, or health food store owner. Or, maybe it just makes sense to you that what nourishes your body can also heal your body. Or, you just know that people ought to have the right to make certain decisions on their own.

Now you can do something. You want to do something real, that will make a dent, and that will help change things. Maybe you will do two things, depending on how determined you become — who knows , this could bring out the activist in you. It sure did with me....

So, what is the single most important thing that you can do? Write a letter. Simply put down on paper what is important to you. Letter writing is the most powerful tool in a democracy. Petitions are not as valuable for several reasons which I will go into shortly. Letters — written to individual lawmakers, typed, handwritten or word processed, with your personal signature and your own words — speak the power of the people.

We have won a crucial victory in achieving the one-year moratorium on FDA enforcement of the nutritional labeling regulations against dietary supplements. It came at the very end of the 102nd congressional session. The Health Freedom bills were introduced too late in the session to gather the broad base of support that they will need in Congress, and this moratorium gives us another year to refine our proposals and achieve our goal. The 1992 elections will bring a huge number of new members to congress. Veterans will shift their places on committees. It is impossible to say at this time exactly how our bills will resurface next session.

Our mission at this time should be to thank those who have supported us this past year and to make new friends. And, as friendship is a person-to-person sort of thing, it requires the personal touch that only a personal letter can bring.

Letters have a beginning (usually the hardest part), a middle, and an end. One page is best. Short is fine, especially when it's to the point. And believe me, you don't have to know a lot of facts because the really important fact is that you are taking the time to write this letter in the first place. Just stick to your story and tell it like it is.

Writing Your Letter, Step-by-Step

In the beginning, say why you are writing to this lawmaker:
- Because I have respected many positions you have taken in the past...
- Because I voted for you...
- Because I didn't vote for you but I will if...
- Because you chair such-and-such committee...
- To thank you for your support...
- Because you have stated your position and I want to change your mind...

In the middle, say why this is important to you:
- I was ill, and not getting better until I used such-and-such...
- I have used this for so many years and have enjoyed such excellent health...
- I think this will save the country money...
- I want to protect the jobs of my employees and benefit society too...
- This is part of my family heritage...
- I believe in this...
- It just makes sense to me that the foods that nourish our bodies can heal them too...
- It does not make sense to stop people from trying, on their own, to stay healthy.

At the end, ask for what you want:
- Please co-sponsor health freedom legislation,
- Please protect my right to get truthful information and make educated choices,
- Please don't give the FDA more power to restrict my choices,
- Please don't give the FDA power to unfairly restrict my business,
- Please investigate the societal benefits of dietary supplements and/or complementary medicine,
- Please protect my civil right to choose what kind of medicine I will use.

You can find your Senators and Representatives listed in the general information of your telephone book, or, call the League of Women Voters. Address your letters to The Honorable so and so. And write again as the situation develops and changes — after all, these guys work for you.

Why are letters better than petitions? Petitions have their place, and they are neat in that you have so many names on one sheet of paper. Petitions are useful in circumstances where there is a proposal put forth that you wish to defeat. Then the petition acts as a referendum. Another time when petitions work is when something has happened that you wish to protest quickly. However, as of October 9, 1992, our position is not so much one of opposition and protest because now we are encouraging positive actions — *sponsorship* of our bills!

It's easier to defeat legislation than achieve legislation. All a law maker has to do to defeat a bill is say "no." But to pass a bill, sponsors must become educated about the facts, convince their colleagues, and sometimes, be willing to give up something else that they, or some of their constituents, might want. Letters are the extra effort that can turn philosophical sympathies into enthusiastic sponsorship, and change opposition into support.

What about form letters? The following is a very personal opinion, which you may take or leave: The form letter message is not personal and yet it takes up a whole sheet of paper. Better to have just signed a petition and saved a tree.

Why not just make a phone call? There is a time and a place for everything, and phone calls certainly have their place. For the most part, I discourage phone calls. Imagine trying to complete your work with the phone constantly ringing. Being dismissed as a nuisance will not help us get what we want. But there are two times when making a phone call is good: 1) When bills are going to a vote in a committee or on the floor (and then you should only call the offices of the people actually voting). 2) To make an appointment for a visit to a lawmaker's office (which you really should consider doing, by the way).

What about an office visit? Good idea. And, between sessions, in the months of November, December and mid-January, are the times to catch your lawmakers at their district offices. Even if you only meet with staff, your message will get to the lawmaker more directly if you visit in the districts during this time. Again the key is to tell your personal story. Not the long telling with the excruciating and thrilling details, but the simple and direct telling, that gets quickly to the crux of why you have come to this office at this time. And, as with all things in life, be sure to ask for what you want.

Protocol for Office Visits

Here are some simple office visit protocol, based on generalizations from lots of visits:

- Introduce everyone in your party with a one line tie-in for each person.
- Quickly introduce the subject of your visit, then move on to the background information (it will make more sense being placed in context this way).
- Acknowledge and address your remarks to any staff present as well, for they will be doing the actual follow-up.
- Avoid getting drawn into discussing details with which you are not familiar It's OK to say "I don't know about that, but what's important to me is..."
- If the lawmaker starts to accept phone calls, your visit is over and you should politely leave.
- Prepare for only a 15 minute meeting and only go longer at the prompting of the lawmaker. Better to have been short

and sweet than be causing inconvenience.
- Find the positive note on which to end your meeting and be sure to shake hands.
- Send a letter to thank the lawmaker for taking the time, giving their attention, etc.

Of the People, For the People

Your role is an important one. You are the citizen, the voter, the "by the people" part of the equation. You are represented by a number of good lobbyists, who study the facts, track the bills' progress, and do the grunt work of education and influence. We present the case "for the people." But we can't do that without you. For in this issue, at this time, the straw that will break the political camel's back is the human factor — you. Your letters will reach out and make contact. Your visits will bring the issue home. Your stories will foster the best quality in any lawmaker, that innocent impulse that inspires him or her to serve, perform and be "of the people."

Good luck! And, just a note of counsel for when you are feeling down and discouraged: Persevere! Although you may feel like your words just went in one ear and out the other, persevere. You are not alone and we won't go away until we have won!

Editor's note: *Please remember that some of the content in this chapter may become obsolete after January 1993; the names and numbers of bills will change, new ones introduced, etc. It is important that you send us the reader-response card in the very front of this book so we can mail you an update when political events call for it.*

How to Stop the FDA

by Bonnie K. and Clinton Ray Miller

The Millers have been full time health freedom lobbyists for the past 30 years. They were instrumental in the passage of the Proxmire Amendments in 1976.

When Congress enacted the National Labeling and Education Act (NLEA) on November 8, 1990, it unknowingly granted the US Food and Drug Administration (FDA) permission to build a new regulatory gallows on which it could hang the leaders of America's alternative health revolution.

For several decades, the FDA has been trying to convince a skeptical Congress that most supplemental vitamins and minerals are not only unnecessary, but present such a serious threat to the nation's health that they should be outlawed unless prescribed by an MD.

In 1962, at the urging of the American Medical Association (AMA), FDA published regulations which would permit it to regulate most vitamins and minerals as drugs. For example, vitamin C in excess of 90 milligrams would only have been available as a prescription drug.

For fourteen years the debate raged. We helped create a powerful national grassroots network and taught thousands of health-conscious consumers how to lobby effectively on a very limited budget. We quickly learned that properly written form letters were the most cost-effective way to get hundreds of thousands of people informed and actively involved in lobbying for their health freedom. As a result, Congress received more mail against the FDA's prescription-vitamin proposal than it received on any issue during that time — except Watergate and the Vietnam War.

Finally, in 1976, Congress responded by *unanimously* enacting the Proxmire vitamin bill. It prohibited the FDA from classifying and then regulating "...any natural or synthetic vitamin or mineral (or combination thereof) as a drug solely because it exceeds the level of potency which..." the FDA had determined "...was nutritionally rational or useful." It was a devastating and humiliating defeat for the FDA and the AMA. Never before in our history has Congress given such a stinging rebuke to a proposal by a government agency. It was one of the greatest legislative miracles of the century. We can repeat it in getting Congress to enact the Hatch/Richardson/Gallegly Health Freedom Acts.

FDA Bureaucrats Don't Repent, They Retrench, Recoil, Plot, Wait, and Strike Again

A few of the FDA's anti-vitamin bureaucrats have learned how to manipulate and mislead some members of Congress. They are patient. Because they are un-elected, they know they can usually outlast most legislators. They decided to wait until Proxmire was defeated or retired before openly attacking vitamins again. They had a long wait. Proxmire could easily have been re-elected until he died, but he decided to retire in 1988 after serving since 1957 and attendings over 10,000 consecutive roll calls.

FDA Asks Congress For More Enforcement Weapons — Waxman Introduces HR 2597

With Proxmire out of the way, the FDA moved quickly. It convinced Senator Metzenbaum (D-OH) and Representative Waxman (D-CA) that the FDA was virtually "helpless" to protect consumers against misbranded or unsafe dietary supplements. Waxman introduced HR 2597 on June 7, 1991, to give the FDA massive new enforcement authority. Then, the NLEA regulations were submitted by the FDA [see chapter by James L. Beck]. Waxman hastily withdrew HR 2597 four months later when it came under heavy attack by our health freedom network; all the Republicans on his subcommittee; several trade associations; thousands of consumers; and a threatened veto by President Bush.

Waxman made several amendments and reintroduced the bill as HR 3642. He was able to get it voted out of the House

Health Subcommittee 13-7 and the Full Committee 27-16 strictly along party lines. Bush still threatened to veto HR 3642 / S 2135.

Senator Edward Kennedy (D-MA) introduced S 2135, a similar companion bill, in the Senate on November 23, 1991. Waxman and Kennedy allowed their bills to "die" at the end of the session but are expected to reintroduce them in the 103rd Congress. They are very bad bills!

How To Lobby For and Against Good and Bad Bills

1. Get a copy of the bill. Any person can get a free copy of a House Bill by calling 202-225-3456. This is the number of the House Document Room in Washington, D.C.
2. Read the bill. Most bills are as easy to read as the newspaper. There will probably be sections you do not fully understand. Feel free to phone the sponsor of the bill and ask the staff person in charge of the bill to send you copies of any press releases or statements made by the sponsor on the bill.
3. Read the criticisms (pro and con) of the bill. You can usually obtain these documents from health freedom advocacy groups such as NCIH [see also a listing of such groups in chapter by Claire Farr]. Once you have determined how you stand on the bill, send personal letters to your legislators. If you agree with the criticism of an advocacy organization, you may wish to consider the convenience of using their form letters. Get as many others as possible to do the same.
4. If you find the criticisms of the bill to be wrong, inaccurate, or unfair, then write or call the health freedom advocacy group to express yourself. They can then reconsider, amend and/or correct their position.
5. Make personal phone calls to your Representative or Senators (or their staff). Each Senator and Representative has a staff person responsible for different legislation or issues. Find out which staff person is responsible for the bill you wish to discuss and talk to them. The phone number for the central congressional switchboard for all members of both Senate and the House is 202-224-3121.
6. Call and/or write your local radio or television talk-show host

and let them know about the bill.
7. Write letters to the editor of your local newspaper.
8. When hearings are held, submit your written testimony to be included in the record.
9. Never threaten. Always be courteous, respectful and kind, but be as persistent as you find is necessary. Don't be afraid to express your thoughts *and* feelings relating to the legislation. Be informed before you call. If you don't know something, admit it rather that pretend that you know.

Sample Form Letters

The following pages have two form letters which we have prepared for your use, one in support of S 2835 (The Health Freedom Act) and one in support of HR 5746 (The Health Choices Freedom Act). You can photocopy these letters from this book, fill in your representative's name, sign them, and mail them in.

Editor's notes: *This and the chapter called "So What's A Person To Do?" by Monica Miller are the most important chapters in this book. They spell out just exactly what you can do to help save your health freedom. Notice how the authors of the two chapters differ on the topic of form letters: Monica feels that they are not effective, while Bonnie and Clinton feel they are. Readers will have to decide for themselves.*

We would like to remind readers that some of the content in this chapter may need to be updated after January 1993; the names and numbers of bills will change, new ones will be introduced, etc. It is important that you send us the reader-response card in the very front of this book so that we can mail you an update when political events dictate.

The Honorable _____
United States Senate
Washington, D.C. 20510   _____
                                                date

Dear Senator _____

I am writing to urge you to support pending health-freedom legislation in the Senate. I am convinced that the FDA's impending NLEA regulations (effective in December of 1993) will allow the FDA to remove all amino acids, most medicinal herbs, and all above-RDA vitamin supplements from the over-the-counter market and turn them into prescription drugs. I do not believe the FDA when they say they they have no intention to do that. Indeed, they have repeatedly tried to do just that in the past.

If the FDA is allowed to proceed with their plans, my pursuit of life, liberty and happiness will be severely restricted. I use these products daily to enhance my health and prevent disease. I am convinced that nutrient supplements are the key to lowering health-care costs and that the FDA's ill-conceived plans, if not revoked, will cost us dearly.

I ask you to support health-freedom legislation that will:
1) define "dietary supplement" as a product intended to add *vitamins, amino acids, minerals, herbs* or other *similar nutritional substances* to our diets.
2) prohibit the FDA from *regulating dietary supplements as drugs*.
3) prohibit the FDA from regulating dietary supplements as *food additives*.
4) remove the FDA's ability to arbitrarily restrict *truthful and non-misleading claims* about the relationship of dietary supplements to health and disease.
5) retain the FDA's ability to prosecute health fraud in *criminal court*.

I believe that this combination of provisions, if enacted and enforced, will 1) protect consumers from fraud, and 2) protect consumers from the FDA. It is simple, inexpensive, and does not require additional bureaucracy.

I would very much like to hear your considerations about the specific health-freedom bills before Congress. Please ask your staff to inform me of your position(s) and which bill(s) you are going to support and co-sponsor.

I feel very strongly about this issue and will be paying close attention to the disposition of these bills in the current Congress.

Sincerely yours,

_____   _____
Print name   Signature

_____
Address (street, city, state, ZIP)

The Honorable _____
United States House of Representatives
Washington, D.C. 20515   _____
                                              date

Dear Representative _____

I am writing to urge you to support pending health-freedom legislation in the House. I am convinced that the FDA's impending NLEA regulations (effective in December of 1993) will allow the FDA to remove all amino acids, most medicinal herbs, and all above-RDA vitamin supplements from the over-the-counter market and turn them into prescription drugs. I do not believe the FDA when they say they they have no intention to do that. Indeed, they have repeatedly tried to do just that in the past.

If the FDA is allowed to proceed with their plans, my pursuit of life, liberty and happiness will be severely restricted. I use these products daily to enhance my health and prevent disease. I am convinced that nutrient supplements are the key to lowering health-care costs and that the FDA's ill-conceived plans, if not revoked, will cost us dearly.

I ask you to support health-freedom legislation that will:
1) define "dietary supplement" as a product intended to add *vitamins, amino acids, minerals, herbs* or other *similar nutritional substances* to our diets.
2) prohibit the FDA from *regulating dietary supplements as drugs*.
3) prohibit the FDA from regulating dietary supplements as *food additives*.
4) remove the FDA's ability to arbitrarily restrict *truthful and non-misleading claims* about the relationship of dietary supplements to health and disease.
5) retain the FDA's ability to prosecute health fraud in *criminal court*.

I believe that this combination of provisions, if enacted and enforced, will 1) protect consumers from fraud, and 2) protect consumers from the FDA. It is simple, inexpensive, and does not require additional bureaucracy.

I would very much like to hear your considerations about the specific health-freedom bills before Congress. Please ask your staff to inform me of your position(s) and which bill(s) you are going to support and co-sponsor.

I feel very strongly about this issue and will be paying close attention to the disposition of these bills in the current Congress.

Sincerely yours,

_____   _____
Print name   Signature

_____
Address (street, city, state, zip)